BENNY

BENNY

THE TRUE STORY

DENNIS KIRKLAND

WITH HILARY BONNER

SMITH GRYPHON
PUBLISHERS

First published in Great Britain in 1992 by
SMITH GRYPHON LIMITED
Swallow House, 11–21 Northdown Street
London N1 9BN

A CIP catalogue record for this book is available from the British Library.

ISBN 1-85685-031-5

Typeset by Computerset, Harmondsworth, Middlesex
Printed by Butler & Tanner Ltd, Frome

CONTENTS

THE BEN I KNEW

The real Benny Hill was a shadowy figure. One minute within your grasp, the next just a fleeting impression in the back of your mind; and if you reached out for him too eagerly he would disappear. Two things I know about him without doubt. He was a great, great comedian. And, to me, an even greater friend.

His death over Easter 1992 was a tragedy, not least because he was on the brink of making his first new TV series in four years. But professionally he will live for ever because, thankfully, there is a full record of his work on film. And I am privileged to have produced and directed so many Benny Hill shows.

Personally Benny was a mystery man, and few people were allowed to become close to him. I believe that I knew him better than anyone alive, and I am always being asked the same questions. How did Benny really live, and why did he live the way he did? If he was so rich, why didn't he buy himself a beautiful home? Why did he never marry? Did he only pretend to love the ladies? Was he a closet homosexual? What was his relationship really like with the Benny

Hill dancers? Did he really carry his money around in plastic carrier bags? Was he mean? What did he do with himself when he wasn't working? Whatever did he do with all that money? What was the truth about that will? What was he really like to work with? And above all, was he really the unhappy man that has been portrayed? Was he sad and lonely?

One of Ben's most successful portrayals was the circus clown. Physically he rather resembled a clown even without make-up. So was that what he was really like? Did he hide a crushed soul and a broken heart behind the mask of those chubby cheeks, the cheeky grin and the twinkly blue eyes?

In these pages I shall answer these questions and many more besides. I want to tell you the kind of man Benny was. I want to share my feelings for him and explain his complex personality as best I can. It is not an easy task, and one that could be aptly accompanied by the haunting theme music from the film *The Third Man* – which, as it happens, was one of Benny's favourite movies. Like the elusive Third Man, just as you think you've got hold of Benny Hill he slips away. He existed in his own special world of make-believe, and I was privileged to be allowed to join him there sometimes.

Benny was unique. He was a one-off who did things his way, and it was sometimes difficult for the rest of us to understand. His idiosyncratic behaviour led to huge misconceptions about Ben. Some of it was his own fault. Here was a man who cared desperately about what the public thought of him. A man who deeply desired not only to be loved and respected but also to be thought of as a nice guy.

The cover of this book shows Benny when he was desperately ill. It was taken just a couple of weeks before his death, on his release from hospital after his first heart attack. Within two hours he was on his way back to hospital. But when he was confronted by photographers outside the hospital he automatically slipped into the character of Fred Scuttle, one of his most long-standing creations, because that was what was expected of him. It was a straightforward human reaction. He accepted that the photographers were waiting there because of the huge public concern over his health, and he wanted to show his fans that he was just fine – even though he was not.

But Benny could never be bothered to play any kind of public relations game. It would not have occurred to him to be part of a contrived campaign to create a certain image in the way favoured by big American stars. To be honest, he was not even capable of it. He even refused point-blank to guest on the big chat shows like *Wogan* and *Aspel*.

When pretending to be someone else he was a great performer. Yet he found it almost impossible to be himself and perform at the same time. Therefore the glimpses the public were given of Benny the private man over the years were frequently misleading. Little has been written about him that has ever come close to the truth.

At work he was a genius. In showbusiness terms it is very simple to sum up Benny Hill. He remains the greatest television comedian ever – nobody has understood and manipulated that medium better or more effectively. Possibly they never will.

It was away from work that the complications began. He was an enigma, a walking paradox. And if I'd said that to him he would have twinkled at me and asked if that was anything to do with the pills he took for his headaches. He was, after all, an old pro stand-up comic weaned in the music halls of another, long-lost Britain. And in the best pro tradition he never missed a gag.

He could be shy. He was very private. He loved to walk, and he loved to walk alone. At home and when he was travelling, walking was his favourite way of getting around; and he used to hope it would help with his constant battle against the flab. He developed a manner of resolute pacing, with his head down and barely looking from side to side, so that he was not easily recognized – so that he could remain in his private little world.

Yet if nobody noticed him he would miss it. He used to think that he just wanted to be left alone, but when he was ignored it made him uneasy. He was a big, big star, and he knew it – of course he knew it. He did not play up to it in the way so many celebrities do. There was no aura about him, and far less of an ego than you will find in most entertainers without the tiniest fraction of the talent of Benny Hill.

A little-known side of Benny was that he spoke at least four languages beautifully and he had learned them all by ear. He never had a lesson, yet was fluent in French, Spanish and German, and I believe he was pretty good at Italian. The reason I'm not sure is because we never went to Italy together, and I only found out the extent of his ability when I visited these various countries with him and had to listen to him jabbering away like a native. All he ever said to me about what was actually a tremendous gift was: 'Oh yes, young Den, I can get my face slapped in half a dozen different languages.'

He nearly got his face slapped once by Blake Edwards, the Hollywood producer married to Julie Andrews. It was years ago, when Benny was still working for the BBC – he was not then known internationally as a comedian, but had started to appear in films. Benny was auditioned by Blake, who wanted him to play a Frenchman in a new movie. Blake asked Benny if he could do a French accent.

'Sure,' replied the young Benny. 'Would you like a Paris accent: East side or West? Or would you rather have a South of France accent – or Marseilles perhaps, or would you prefer the Camargue?'

Blake Edwards was not impressed. 'Mr Hill, God hates a smart arse,' he said, and kicked our hero out the door. It was probably as good a put-down as Benny ever had. But he had not meant to be flash – he really could do all those accents.

He was an extremely clever man, but he had no need to let you know it all the time. In fact, just the opposite. He was, by and large, a modest sort of chap, and remained throughout his life, I think, the same kind of person he had always been – even when he became so incredibly famous worldwide. He didn't change much, which is one of the reasons why he saw no need to change his lifestyle just because he had the money to do so.

His philosophy of living was that you could only sit in one chair at a time. I would also say that you could only eat one meal at a time, but in his case that probably wasn't true. He loved his food so much.

Benny considered himself a perfectly normal, ordinary sort of guy and saw nothing odd about the way he lived. The world expected him to live in the grand style of other multi-millionaires, and because he didn't he was labelled eccentric. Benny couldn't understand it. He didn't think he was eccentric. He just did what he wanted. He was his own man and rarely compromised over anything. He allowed himself few of the trappings of fame and fortune – not because he was mean, but because he didn't care. He did not need or want much more than a warm, comfortable room with a bed and a TV set. He didn't need or want a retinue of lackeys around him responding to his every whim.

When he travelled, he did so without fuss. Nobody checked out the hotel he had booked into to make sure his room was just right and that the staff knew he was arriving and would behave with a suitable display of adoration. But Benny both accepted and expected constant attention as part of his daily life. He knew when he booked into a hotel that he would promptly be moved to the best room in the house as soon as it was realized just who Mr B. Hill was. One half of him did not want to be recognized wherever he went and lamented the loss of privacy. The other half, full of the fear of failure experienced by all comics, panicked when that recognition was not there.

And so it was when Benny eventually made his first trip to America. He was already huge in the States, but, much as he loved to travel, we couldn't get him to go. He was afraid. People told him how big he was but he couldn't quite believe it. After all, this was the country of his boyhood heroes, the land of Hollywood whence came those wonderful movies which had spawned Benny's earliest showbiz dreams. He was over-awed. Could he really be a star in America? Surely not!

In 1980 and 1981 *The Benny Hill Show* was nominated for American Emmy awards – the TV equivalent of an Oscar and a rare honour for a British show – but he wouldn't even fly over for the award ceremonies. Then one day out of the blue he phoned me up and said he would like to go to America at last. 'I want to suss it out quietly, see how the land lies,' he said. 'I just want to see if it really is the way everyone tells me it is over there with the show.' He asked me to go with him and, of course, I gladly agreed.

We flew to San Francisco incognito. I had told Thames Television about the trip and they sent me to represent them officially in case there were any interviews or press calls. 'Oh, there won't be,' I said confidently. 'Benny wants to keep this jaunt very quiet. If he's happy, he'll go on a promotional trip another time.'

'I don't want anyone to know I'm going to be there, little heart,' he had said to me. 'Please, no publicity. Don't tell the world I'm coming.'

So I abided by his wishes. I didn't tell anybody. That was my first mistake.

The Taffner organization, who market Benny's shows in America for Thames, knew he was coming because Benny wanted to check out what was going on and have talks with them. But they too had been sworn to secrecy and they totally honoured Benny's wishes.

After two days in San Francisco Benny had been recognized a couple of times in the street but that was all. He had been doing his usual trick of walking around everywhere with his head down. And it worked. People didn't catch his eye and didn't recognize him. So he had got his wish, his visit was totally private, and he should have been very happy. But, of course, he wasn't.

On the third morning he phoned from his hotel room to mine. 'Have the press been on to you at all, Den?' he asked, ever so casually.

'Nope,' I said. 'Not a whisper.'

There was a pause. 'Uh, do you think we'd better have a press call, young Den?'

'OK. If you want one.'

I organized it. The next day everyone knew he was in town and he was mobbed wherever he went. He had been adamant that he wanted no publicity, but, boy, did he hate it when he didn't get any.

Another Benny peculiarity was this total fear he had of any kind of authority. I think it had been instilled in him as a child and he never lost it. It was that extreme respect for people in certain positions in society that we all used to be taught as children, and most of us got over quite quickly. But Benny never did. Policemen, solicitors, doctors and lawyers all came into this category for him.

I remember many times being in his flat when the phone rang, and if it was, say, his doctor I would know at once. If Benny was standing up he would not stand up straight. He would slightly crouch over the phone as if he had been caught misbehaving and was up in front of the headmaster. The body language was fascinating. It was all 'I'm ever so sorry, sir, I didn't mean to kick my ball over the wall. It wasn't really my fault and I *am* sorry, sir.' In fact throughout his life he had that reluctance to bother his doctor if he felt poorly. Even at the end that was true. He had a tight feeling in his chest and he had convinced himself it was the flu. He had to be bullied into going to the doctor. It's the same attitude that I remember from my mum and dad when I was a boy. If Benny was ill over a weekend he would always wait till Monday. And then he'd probably say: 'I'll just give it until tomorrow and see if I feel any better.'

If he phoned his solicitor he would stumble and stutter on the phone, full of uncertainty. 'Uh, hello. Yes. Um. I'm sorry to disturb you. But it's Benny Hill here, and I just wondered, um, uh . . .' and so on. It used to tickle me pink actually. Here was this megastar who was one of the few people in the world who could buy out almost any firm of solicitors, buy himself a helicopter to the best hospital in the country and then maybe buy that as well – and yet he behaved like a naughty schoolboy with these people. They were figures of authority representing part of his past and they made him nervous. Extraordinary but true.

Going through customs with Benny was hilarious. These guys in uniforms were a real threat to him for no reason at all. Benny would not have dreamed of bringing a packet of chewing gum into the country if it was one packet more than was allowed. He used to buy a few presents as a rule. There would be maybe a couple of bottles of perfume for the girls in the show, and something for the guys – some cigars for Henry McGee and perhaps a bottle of brandy for Bob Todd. But that was enough to make him fret about whether or not he was within the rules.

He knew that I never bought anything except a present for my daughter, and he used to get me to carry half the stuff through customs for him. I would tell him he was well inside the limits, which he invariably was, but he would take no chances with authority ever.

When we collected our luggage I used to sit him in a corner and pick up his bags as well as mine. I always did that after the time he got into such a panic trying to grab my suitcase that he ripped his hand open and nearly ended up in hospital – probably because he was working up to a nervous breakdown before going through customs. And so he would sit very quietly, head down, and on these occasions genuinely hope nobody would recognize him and start queueing for autographs. He'd be quiet as a mouse, trying desperately to disappear into the background. Then I'd turn up with a loaded trolley and off we'd go towards the green gate.

As we approached that 'Nothing to Declare' sign he underwent a personality change. He used to get busier and busier and his little feet would be going faster and faster. He would start to talk very, very loudly about absolutely nothing at all. 'Is your wife meeting you, Den? Oh, my word, she'll probably be outside waiting, then. And you have got that present for Joanna haven't you? Oh, jolly good.' What he was really saying was: 'Look at me, I'm being dead ordinary, everyone, aren't I?'

I used to look at him and think: 'Who *are* you being?'

In the many times I travelled with Benny all over the world he was never once stopped by customs when I was with him. It might have been because they recognized him as Benny Hill. More probably it was because nobody who was really carrying anything they shouldn't would ever make quite so much a pillock of themselves, I am sure of that.

If they had opened his suitcase they would have found a couple of shirts, the usual toothbrush and razor, a few old socks and Benny's inevitable clutter of papers, scribbled notes, magazines, old news-papers covered in jottings, half-written letters and all the rest of the stuff he always had with him. None the less, Benny was always full of guilt when confronted with customs. And it transformed him into a nervous wreck.

Policemen turned him to stone. Once I was driving Benny home after rehearsals and as we were going through the lovely Bushey Park not far from his Teddington flat we were stopped by the park police. Now my car is a real old banger and I am not a good car keeper. The floor and the back seat are all covered in old cigarette packets and newspapers, half torn-up maps, and goodness knows what else.

Most big stars of Benny's calibre wouldn't have gone near the old wreck. They would have insisted in travelling in a Roller or a stretch limo or something. Benny couldn't have cared less. He liked my company, so he rode in my car. On this occasion he regretted it.

The policeman walked menacingly around my bashed up motor and announced that I did not appear to have a tax disc.

Earlier that day I had given a lift to Bob Todd, one of Ben's regular supporting cast in the show, and it always took him for ever to get in and out of a car – during which time everything around would be tossed in all directions.

So at once I said: 'Oh, God. Toddy must have knocked it onto the floor. Benny, would you mind getting out?'

By this time the copper had his notebook ready and his pencil aimed. Benny got out of the car very quietly, head down, clutching the inevitable supermarket carrier bag – which, I will reveal, did not contain a fortune in used tenners but usually the night's supper and his scripts and notes.

Benny was mortified. There was a grassy bank sloping away from the road and he trotted down it and stood in the long grass trying hard not to be noticed. Plastic bag still in hand. Head right down. The schoolboy in front of the headmaster again.

Of course I could not find this tax disc anywhere. No chance. Eventually Benny looked up to take a peek at what was going on. Then the policeman recognized him. You could see the expression changing on his face. 'Oh my God, I'm nicking Benny Hill!'

At about that time, while scrabbling amongst all the rubbish in the back of my car, I came up with a couple of rubber truncheons. I handed one to the copper and hit myself over the head with the other. Benny was just totally dismayed. Down went the head again. We were in all this serious trouble, and all I could do was camp it up with a rubber truncheon. He looked as if he wanted the ground to open up and swallow him. I shall remember for the rest of my life the picture of this multi-millionaire superstar standing in a foot of wet grass with his head bowed, absolutely terrified because a policeman had stopped my car.

Probably due to Benny, I shouldn't wonder, I was despatched with a caution and an order to take my tax disc to my local police station when I did manage to find the thing.

So Benny climbed back into the car, and his shoes were wet through. But there was no way he could have stood on the road anywhere near what was happening between me and that copper.

He had not said a word throughout the incident and as we drove along he did not speak for quite a long time.

Then he said, quietly: 'You have got a tax disc, haven't you, Den?'

I couldn't resist it. 'No,' I said casually.

But he looked so absolutely shocked and horrified that I quickly had to relent. 'It's all right,' I assured him. 'Of course I've got one. Somewhere . . . .'

And so you get a picture of a timid man. But he could be a complete monster when he was working. Then he was totally in charge. Then he would always know what was right and what was wrong. And you couldn't even argue with him most of the time, because he was almost always right. He was a perfectionist. And he was good. But something else that stayed with him was a sense of wonderment at his own level of success.

Once we were at a TV festival in Cannes in the South of France where we had been to a lavish lunch thrown by Thames. We had a couple of hours to ourselves and had been told that the next day would be free. As ever, Benny had been to the South of France many, many times and knew all the best places and the top hotels, whereas I had never been before. He couldn't wait to show me around, and he planned to do it in style. He had been given a chauffeur-driven Mercedes for the duration of his stay, and that helped with the style quite a bit.

We had had a really marvellous lunch, so Benny said: 'Come on. Let's walk it off. Let's walk along the prom.'

Off we set in the sunshine. There were beautiful girls on the beach, pretty buildings on the other side of the road – it was before the French pulled most of the loveliest in Cannes down – and all the people were calling: 'Benny! Benny!'

It was a good day. There we were with lovely fat bellies full of lobster and champagne, and Benny started to plan what we should do with our free day.

'I'll tell you what – you don't know this area at all, do you?' he asked.

'No,' I said.

'Right, then, little heart. I'll tell you what we'll do tomorrow. We'll get the chauffeur to take us out and we'll run over to Nice, and we'll have a look around and a couple of jars in a bar on the front, then we'll get back in the car and we'll drive to Juan les Pins for lunch on the beach. You'll like that . . . . All right?'

'That sounds fine, Ben,' I said.

'Right, then. When we've done that, when we've had lunch, when you're ready, when you're quite sure you're ready, we'll get the chauffeur to run us to Monte Carlo, stopping off wherever you feel like, whenever you like. OK?'

'Sounds fine, Ben,' I said.

'Then I'll show you Monte Carlo. You'll love it. And I'll take you to one of the best restaurants in the world for dinner.'

'Well, yeah, Ben, but what about the Nelsons?' I asked. Nelson Eddies – readies: Cockney rhyming slang for money.

He waved his hand at me dismissively. 'Forget about the Nelsons. I'll do all that . . . . So, then when we've had dinner I'll take you up to the Casino and you'll play all the tables. Anything you like. I'll give you the money to play the tables. OK?'

'Sounds great, Ben,' I said. And I was thinking to myself, this is the man they call mean?

'Right, then. After that we'll go to see the show, because you've got to see the show at the Casino. It's great. Then after that we'll go backstage and we'll meet whoever the star is and we'll meet all the girls, and have a few bottles of champagne. When you've had enough, just say so. We'll get the chauffeur to whisk us back to our five star hotel on the beach at Cannes. How's that for tomorrow?'

'That's all right,' I said.

There was a pause. His eyes were just one big twinkle.

'Not bad for an ex-milkman and a little Geordie, is it?'

I loved that. And I guess what I want to do more than anything else in this book is to try to present the real Benny Hill, just how he was, and to show why I loved him so much.

FROM JACKO TO OLD BLUE EYES

The stars of the showbusiness world certainly loved Benny Hill. It was not only other comedians who recognized and worshipped his talent: some of the biggest celebrities in the world are Benny Hill fans. These include probably the number one of them all – Michael Jackson.

And Michael Jackson did not just worship from afar. Not long before Ben died, Michael visited him in hospital. I was there, and it was an occasion I shall always remember.

Benny's face was a picture. Chubby pink cheeks, sparkling blue eyes, lips puckered into a cheeky grin. He was all a-twinkle. It was typical Ben. Ben at his uniquely funny, magical best. The Ben I had grown to love and admire and know so well. And this was one of the most extraordinary days of his extraordinary life. From his hospital ward he was making plans for a staggering double act. Predictably, just a visit from Michael Jackson was not enough for Benny. Within minutes he was on the verge of doing a deal to make a video film with the guy.

Ben was being treated for his first heart attack. He looked the same as ever. Pink and glowing. That plump face miraculously unlined after sixty-eight years of hard work and – contrary to many misguided reports about him – plenty of hard play.

He was in fact sicker than anybody realized. But, wow, was he enjoying himself! There sitting opposite him on a hard wooden chair in his private hospital room was Michael Jackson. *The* Michael Jackson. The famous reclusive one. The one who doesn't like people to get too close to him. Jackson's much-discussed face was split by a soppy grin as he gazed adoringly at my old pal from behind his regulation protective fringe of entwined black locks.

Ben, up and dressed in a clean shirt and his smartest trousers, silky white hair slicked down for the occasion, sat in the only easy chair. He always had a degree of modesty rare indeed in showbusiness. He was unassuming in manner and not given to self-congratulation. On this occasion, however, the only word I could think of to describe Ben aptly was 'smug'. And I think he could be forgiven. Hospital visits from Michael Jackson are not exactly handed out with the daily medicine.

And Jackson appeared to be mesmerized. He remains arguably the biggest star in the world. He is hero-worshipped by hundreds of millions. His wealth would make Benny – who died worth a staggering £7.5 million – look like a pauper. But Michael Jackson's hero was Benny Hill. Jackson may be the number one superstar. Benny Hill was probably the most popular comedian in the world. And Michael Jackson loved him.

It was always difficult for me to remember, day by day, how important, how very big internationally, Ben had become. To me he was just a best mate. The guy I worked with, drank with and travelled the world with. And here he was with Michael Jackson gazing adoringly at him and generally behaving like a big soft puppy dog.

I heard myself suggest that they should make a film together. Michael Jackson jumped at the idea. It was incredible. He was almost begging Benny. 'I don't believe it. Will you do it, will you really do it, Ben?' he kept saying.

Benny was at his most benign. 'Of course I will, little heart,' he said. 'Why ever not?'

I doubt if anybody had ever called Michael Jackson 'little heart' before. He was loving every minute of it. Suddenly they were planning this video film. The idea was that we would film Michael – who, of course, is such a beautiful dancer – dancing very, very slowly, alongside Benny dancing as fast as possible. Then we would double the speed of the film so that Michael would look normal and Benny would look like 100 miles an hour.

The idea had Michael doubled up with laughter. He kept saying to Benny, 'God, you're so funny. You are *so* funny.' Benny would make some terrible pun and Michael Jackson was virtually rolling on the floor. It was quite a sight. He told us that he had collected videos of virtually every TV show Benny had made, and kept them in a special room. 'I watch them all the time, I have a beautiful room full of your work,' he said.

Michael was so familiar with the shows that he was able to quote sketches at us and tell Benny jokes. He even gave a Fred Scuttle salute. I have no doubt at all that if Benny had lived he and Michael Jackson would have made that film together. And what a double act they would have been.

Michael had been a fan for many years. I know that he had written to Benny through his agent and said he would like to meet him one day, and invited Benny to stay with him in Los Angeles. It was just coincidence that Michael happened to be in London, staying at the Dorchester Hotel, when Benny was in hospital. He decided he would like to visit his hero, and the way that visit came about is quite a story, one which will haunt my twelve-year-old daughter Joanna for many years to come.

Michael got my phone number from somewhere, I don't know where, and telephoned my home one Friday evening. My wife and I were out and Joanna took the call. But she never realized who she was speaking to – which for a great Jacko fan was just devastating.

All the time that Benny was ill the phone in the Kirkland household was just red-hot. Jo spoke to someone called Michael Jackson, and took his name and number. It did not occur to her that the man she was talking to could possibly have been *the* Michael Jackson. She was so unimpressed that she even forgot to give me the message. The entire British press corps, the world and his wife, were all trying to get to Michael Jackson that week. Yet he had left me his private phone number and I didn't even know, thanks to my dozy daughter.

I have to admit, you don't imagine Michael Jackson himself picking up the phone and dialling a number and calling anybody. After all, he travels everywhere with a huge entourage of people to do everything for him.

But the next morning the phone rang about ten o'clock and there was nobody giving me the 'I have a call for you . . .' routine. Instead a familiar voice said: 'Hello, Mr Kirkland. You're a very hard man to get hold of.'

I think I knew immediately who it was. But, Benny-trained as I am in a gag for every occasion, an old favourite just tripped off the tongue. 'No I'm not, ask the wife,' I said.

Fortunately it didn't put him off. I'm not sure that he even heard it really. He just said he had left his private number for me because he wanted to come and see Benny.

I was knocked out. I told him that was great, and then I asked him not to go to the hospital until about one because I wanted to be there as well and couldn't get there earlier than that.

In fact I was fibbing. I phoned Uncle Ben to warn him, and he was thrilled to bits. None the less I rushed along at midday to make sure that he was up with his shirt on and his hair combed. I later learned that Michael Jackson had actually arrived early and, being the polite chap that he is, had got his chauffeur to drive him around the block for three-quarters of an hour so that he would arrive dead on time.

Anyway, quite oblivious of all this I was busily making sure Ben was ready and comfortable and all of that, and at about a quarter past twelve decided to go to the pub for half an hour. 'All right, little sausage,' said Ben.

I opened the door to Ben's room and outside his door were six Mike Tysons, just standing there. Well, that's how they seemed to me at my height of five foot eight. They were the kind of guys who stand as if they have boils under their arms. They were kitted out with radios, and I didn't know if they had guns or not, but you didn't feel inclined to give them occasion to demonstrate.

'Who are you?' they demanded, and they had voices that came out of their boots.

I told them and they were ultra-courteous. 'Oh yes, Mr Kirkland, we've been told to find you,' they said.

Now I reckoned this could be a mixed blessing. Surprisingly, I discovered the courage to ask them who they were.

'We are Michael Jackson's front guard,' they explained. 'We go ahead to make sure there is no trouble.'

I looked at them all lined up in the corridor and assured them there would be no trouble.

And spot on one, in came Michael Jackson. You hear all the stories about him and how he has done terrible things to his face, but his behaviour was sweet and charming and really quite normal. 'Do you want a Coca Cola?' asked Ben. And then before Jackson could answer he added: 'Oh crikey, no. It's Pepsi you support, isn't it?' Because we knew Pepsi Cola would be sponsoring his European tour later in the year, as they do almost every Michael Jackson project.

Michael giggled at everything. About every ten minutes one of his minders would come in and tell him it was time to go – obviously a pre-arranged thing. But each time Michael sent him away, saying, 'It's OK. I'm all right.'

It was a curious experience for me. There I was in a hospital bedroom with two of the richest and most famous men in the world, and I needed to get away because I had to go to sign on the dole. Times had been hard for me since Benny's show was dropped by Thames, and I was due to sign on at my local Department of Health and Social Security Office to collect my unemployment money. Now how do you explain that to a pair of multi-millionaires?

Michael Jackson was in no hurry. He was with Ben for more than fifty minutes. And apparently Michael never spends that long with anyone. But Ben had that effect on people. He had many famous fans. They read like a list out of a showbusiness *Who's Who*.

A lot of Hollywood actors, including Clint Eastwood and Burt Reynolds, are great devotees. Clint has written him lots of letters, and on our first trip to America together the Taffner organization threw a party for Ben in Los Angeles to which they invited Clint and a whole host of other stars. Clint, who was in Las Vegas at the time, phoned us at our hotel to ask if he could bring along his son Kyle, a lovely big lad just like his dad. Clint used to have pictures of Benny all over his restaurant. He loved him. Ultimately he couldn't get back from Vegas that time, but he always kept in touch. And Benny met Clint's son many times. We had more success with Burt Reynolds, and we enjoyed a night out with Burt and the comedy actor Dom De Luise. Burt adored Ben, and it was great fun. A real boozy boy's night out.

The next day – very much the morning after – Hugh Hefner, the legendary Playboy boss, had invited us to a party at his mansion in Los Angeles. I will never forget it for a number of reasons. Hefner was hysterical. He greets everyone in black silk pyjamas. It's all part of his image. And, of course, there were beautiful girls everywhere.

But before you get to the pyjamas or the girls you have to negotiate a talking rock and a terrifying team of security men. Hefner lives in probably the best guarded house in LA, and you play it by the rules when you get to visit him.

Benny and I bowled up in a taxi and we were told: 'Talk to the rock and whatever you do don't back off.' Well, of course, you get there, and the gate doesn't look like a gate, and you can't believe you have to talk to this rock, and Ben and I weren't at our best, and the next thing that happened was that our driver slammed the car into reverse and backwards we shot – which on a bad day could get you shot outside the Hefner house. These huge black-suited blokes came out of nowhere and this time there was no mistake – they were tooled up all right. We had backed off. If you back off there's something wrong. And these guys looked ready for action.

I was screaming at the driver: 'Talk to the rock! Talk to the rock!' Benny seemed to find it all very funny. Maybe it was nerves.

Eventually the driver spoke to the rock and told the rock who he had aboard. And the rock answered, and suddenly everything was OK. It's so camp, no wonder Benny couldn't stop laughing. Then the doors opened like the parting of the Red Sea and there was the feel of a miracle about it.

Inside there was Hefner in his pyjamas. He took us to the bar and spent about forty-five minutes talking to Ben and telling him how great he was. Just like Michael Jackson, minders kept turning up to tell the great man the time. He took no notice, which caused a deal of consternation because apparently Hugh Hefner never spends more than five minutes – top whack – with anybody.

But he couldn't stop talking to Ben. Finally Hefner went upstairs with this gorgeous blonde lady and we thought, well, this is what is supposed to happen here. This certainly fits the image. We had another drink and a bit of a giggle, and then five minutes later Hefner came running to the top of the stairs and shouted: 'Benny, Benny, they're taking the micky out of you on *The Johnny Carson Show*.' So America's most famous ladykiller had actually been watching TV with his gorgeous blonde – and was confronted with Benny Hill yet again.

It turned out that Burt Reynolds and Dom De Luise were on *The Johnny Carson Show*, and telling the story of us lot on the town the night before. As we toured from bar to bar, Burt had come up with this gag about these four guys who couldn't find a bird between the four of them – so we took it in turns to wear a frock to cheer each other up. And he told the tale on *Carson*.

Well, it was funny at the time anyway. I was less amused when Benny later confessed to me that he had turned down an invitation from Frank Sinatra in order to visit Hugh Hefner. Sinatra is another great Benny Hill fan. Once, when he flew into Britain on a singing tour, he announced: 'I want to do two things here. I want to sing with the London Philharmonic Orchestra and I want to go to a Benny Hill rehearsal.'

Sadly, it wasn't possible at the time because we weren't rehearsing. So when Old Blue Eyes heard we were in Hollywood he phoned Benny in his hotel room. Now all Benny's calls were transferred to me, but because it was Sinatra they put him straight through and he told Ben he would like to fly him to Las Vegas. 'I would love to meet you and I want you to be my guests at my show,' he said. The date clashed with the Hefner do, and so Benny told Sinatra he couldn't make it. 'Some other time,' they agreed casually. I was absolutely sick when I learned this. If the call had come though to me I would have cancelled Hefner at a 100 miles an hour. What could be more exciting than to go to Vegas as guests of Frank Sinatra?

Ben just smiled wickedly. 'Oh, little heart. Think of all those girls we would have missed . . . .' That was the Benny Hill image, of course. But also it was not Benny's style to cancel an arrangement once he had made it. Like Michael Jackson, Benny Hill was naturally a courteous man.

His fans came from all walks of life, all countries and all age groups. Mickey Rooney called him a genius. Michael Caine, with whom he starred in *The Italian Job*, also saw Ben as a genius. We met Audrey Hepburn at an awards dinner in New York, and she and Ben competed with each other about which had earned least in London theatre forty-five years earlier. She then gave the photographers her card and asked them to send her the pictures of her with Ben. 'So that my sons will believe me,' she said.

And I discovered recently that Jason Donovan is one of Benny's most devoted fans. The former *Neighbours* star, who was such a big hit in the lead role of the Andrew Lloyd Webber musical *Joseph and His Amazing Technicolour Dreamcoat* at The London Palladium, became a devotee back home in his native Australia.

'I was brought up on Benny Hill,' he says. 'He is huge in Australia, and when I was a boy his TV shows were something you never missed. Everything stopped in our house for Benny Hill.'

Jason had a particular reason for becoming a big Benny fan. His mother, Sue Macintosh, an Australian TV announcer, was once a Benny Hill chorus girl in the fifties when he was with the BBC. In those days she was Sue Menlove – a name Benny would not have been able to resist.

Perhaps the greatest accolade to Benny from his peers was that he was also much loved and admired by the other first-division British comedians of his generation. Men like Les Dawson, Ken Dodd and Bruce Forsyth were all Benny Hill fans. They also envied him. Many of them tried to break into the American market and none of them succeeded. Not a single one of Benny's big British comic contemporaries found international fame as he did.

Eric Morcambe once phoned Benny to tell him the story of a trip to Florida. 'You're getting on my nerves, Benny,' he said. 'Everywhere I bloody went, there were these bumper stickers saying: "We love Benny Hill." And T-shirts saying: "We understand Fred Scuttle." I'm fed up with it, I am.'

His partner Ernie Wise, a frequent visitor to America, also joined in the joke – at least Ben was pretty sure it was a joke. 'I've just been trying to get a drink in Fort Lauderdale and it was closed because *The Benny Hill Show* was on the air,' he said. 'You couldn't get a cup of tea, you couldn't get a glass of wine. You could get nothing because they were all watching blessed Benny Hill. One day somebody in a bar turned to me and said, "You're English, do you know Benny

Hill?" So I gave in. "He's one of my nearest and dearest mates," I said. They all went "What!" And suddenly I could get all the drinks I wanted. So thank you for that at least, Ben.'

When they were both starting out, Bob Monkhouse and Benny launched an on-air sparring match in which they relentlessly poked fun at each other. It was a clever piece of mutual plugging aimed at boosting both careers. Bob called Ben Fanny Hill's son, after the famous fictional Victorian prostitute, and Ben called Bob Blob Monkhouse. After a while Benny just stopped taking part. Without warning, he pulled out of the game. Showing great generosity towards another performer, Bob says that Ben was moving on to a whole new level; he realized this, and wanted to disassociate himself from other comedians.

Bob bore no resentment. 'He was quite right,' he said.

That little story bears testimony to Ben's single-mindedness. And this book will further demonstrate that he did not achieve his unique position worldwide by any kind of accident. His tremendous talent is still there on film, thank God, for all of us to see for ourselves. But Ben knew from the start, as do all true high fliers, that talent alone is rarely enough.

You have to use that talent relentlessly as a tool to further your purpose. You must be prepared to be ruthless, with yourself as well as with others. If you want to get to the very top, if you are an athlete and you want an Olympic Gold, if you are a politician and you want to be President, if you are a curate and you want to be Archbishop, then you must be prepared to sacrifice everything else in your life to that aim. The athlete may speak of his love for his sport, the politician of his mission to change the world, the clergyman of his love for God – but the desire of each to reach the top of their own particular pillar of dreams is actually the true driving force.

So it is if you are a comedian and you want to conquer the world the way Benny Hill did. Do not be fooled by the remembered cuddliness. Benny's whole life was lived according to a master plan which governed everything that he did. Bob Monkhouse said, he knew where he was going. And he was determined to stay there. He never strayed from that path, and he was always totally uncompromising. His fellow stars recognized that in him and it was for all of those reasons – as well as for his talent – that they respected him so much.

Being talented does not make it easier. Nurturing that talent, realizing it to its true potential, driving it mercilessly to glorious fruition – that can be much harder than having no talent at all. And who in the world could understand that better than Michael Jackson, a man who changed his entire persona in pursuit of perfection.

THREE

BENNY AND ME – THE BEGINNING

The first time I ever saw Benny Hill was on television. I was eight years old and one of a family of eight. My father was a factory nightwatchman, and money was short. We lived on a Tynemouth council estate in the industrial north-east of England. There was just one TV on the whole estate. Television was still new and priced out of reach of the vast majority, and certainly way beyond our means. That one set was owned by the people who lived opposite us. They were called the Curries – curiously, the same name as the big British TV store chain in whose shop windows Benny himself first watched TV when he could not afford a set either.

The Curries were our friends. When the TV arrived in their house they became everybody's friends, and the Curries' two girls were the most popular girls on the whole estate. They lived absolutely straight across the street from us, and all the windows roughly matched up, so I was able to peep through both sets of windows at this blue flickering thing. Television sets were always blue in those days. And they always flickered.

One night I caught a glimpse of the *Saturday Night* BBC show, and there was this chubby-faced bloke wearing a little white wig. There was something about him that attracted me even from that distance. I walked across the street and got myself invited into the Curries' much sought-after front room. All the armchairs were taken by the family's fast-expanding circle of dearest friends, and I sat on the floor in the near darkness. The room was lit only by the TV set's eerie flicker. That was quite essential then, of course. The picture was usually so bad that if you had the light on you couldn't see anything at all.

I sat with my legs crossed in front of me staring transfixed at the little miracle in the corner and watched this bloke singing madrigals. His eyes were twinkling and he said something about somebody's dumplings boiling over which became the bane of Benny's life ever after, really. He was always in trouble over his dumpling jokes. I had never heard of Benny Hill and I didn't have a clue who he was. But I thought he was hysterical. And from the beginning he was just made for television. He seemed to be instinctively a TV animal.

The first time I ever met him was at ATV. I was twenty-two years old and a very new assistant floor manager – the next thing up from the call boy and far too lowly to have much to do with Benny, who was already very important. My only dialogue with him was along the lines of, 'Yes, Mr Hill. No, Mr Hill. Ready when you are, Mr Hill. Would you like a cup of tea, Mr Hill?'

Impressive stuff! None the less, Benny always maintained that he remembered me from then, although I never believed him. I certainly remembered him. I watched and learned a lot. He invented the use of split screens and all manner of fascinating technical tricks in comedy. I watched him, and thought what a clever little bugger he was.

Everything that he did was very new and very exciting. Benny was such an innovator. Very early on he started doing badly edited film sketches where you cut bits out and the storyline jumps all over the place. You do a speech and you say a line and you cut out several seconds of it, so you jump about in the way a bad film really does sometimes. Benny might say: 'Yes, it would titillate her.' Which is fine. OK. Nothing wrong with that. But suddenly all you get is: 'Yes, it would tit . . . her.' Typical Hill innuendo, his stock in trade from the start. The viewer knew exactly what was going on because he would jump from one side of the screen to the other. I wasn't involved in it, but I watched, and I thought: 'Ooh, you *are* clever.'

A sketch like one which he did at Thames before I was his director was recently shown again on British TV. It was a *Now Voyager*-type sequence aboard ship, in which Benny and the other performers all spoke out of synch and their dialogue jerked crazily along in such a disjointed way that Ben appeared to tell the lady he was wooing that she was pathetic and she told him she had had her behind for some time. Lovely, mad stuff.

Lew Grade was the first man to make colour TV in England. And so at ATV we had colour cameras shooting for America alongside the black and white ones for home transmission, because there was still no colour TV in Britain and there were different light systems. We did a show called *Spotlight* which was very American-orientated, and the big international stars came trooping into ATV at Elstree. Benny was a regular guest among the likes of Sammy Davis Junior and Sinatra. In fact, Sinatra probably saw Benny for the first time at ATV, although I don't know if he would have remembered. It was much later that he became a Benny Hill fan. And although Benny was already a very famous English comedian, he wasn't in the same league as these people. To Sinatra and Co. he was just the resident home-produced comic among all the big American stars.

I still remember the sketch he did which more than anything else made me realize what a huge talent he had. And this wasn't a particularly TV-orientated one. It was a sketch about Lady Godiva, in which Benny was offered a job as a groom in the famous aristocrat's yard. He would have to muck out the stables and groom the horses and clean up after everyone, and he didn't much like the sound of this job at all. He didn't like the smell and he didn't like the horses much either. Then gradually he realized that Lady Godiva was going to get on a horse naked and ride through the town. Boy, did he want this job suddenly! And that was when I noticed his eyes. The eyes were really going. The twinkle was in overdrive. All of Benny's talent was in his eyes.

The first time I worked properly with Ben was when I joined Thames TV as a floor manager, to which I had been upgraded. I became floor manager of *The Benny Hill Show* a week into rehearsals of the very first one for Thames. When I walked into the rehearsal room Benny was all on his own in the corner. I remember it so well. He was figuring out a Marcel Marceau mime about a man trapped in a balloon, and he was doing this terrible, awful ballet.

It was meant to be bad, and it was so beautifully bad that I just started to fall about. Ben looked up and saw me laughing and said: 'Oh, we'll keep him.' That's exactly what he said, and those were his first real words to me. I just burst out laughing because he looked so brilliant. And from that moment on we got on like a house on fire.

It was the director, John Robins, who had hired me. And he and Benny well and truly lumbered me in the very first week. At the last moment they told me I was doing the warm-up. So out I walked in front of this audience without a clue what I was going to say.

Studio audiences are always given a warm-up man to cheer things up and get them going, of course. Usually he is a professional comic. There are one or two around who make a very good living at it, more or less permanently employed by the TV companies. I'd already done hundreds of shows as floor manager and I was pretty familiar with this routine. So I was surprised to be told that there would be no warm-up man for *The Benny Hill Show*.

John explained to me that, because there were so many inserts and clips and curious technical bits, he and Benny didn't want anybody going out there first and telling a lot of jokes and pulling stunts. It might upset things. 'So on the night,' says John to me, 'I want you to go out and introduce me and I'll come on. I'll do all the business . . . introduce Benny. And all of that. He'll do a bit. Then we'll get on with the show. OK?'

'OK,' I said.

But on the big night, about half an hour before the show started, John Robins said: 'Now, Dennis. Remember what happens. You're going to go out and you're going to do about ten or twelve minutes because you are very funny.'

I went cold. 'What!' I yelled. John just carried on as if I had not spoken. '. . . just introduce me. I'll take a bow and then you do all the business . . . just a bit of an act. Then you carry on and do all the bits in between, when there are stops and starts and things.'

My brain turned to jelly. I started to wobble. I told him I had never done a warm-up in my life. He ignored me. Benny later told me that the whole thing had been as much his idea as John's. I could imagine him sitting in his dressing room waiting to start work and being much cheered up by the thought of the state I was in.

I didn't see Benny after the show that first night. But when we went back to work the following Monday morning he called me over and said I'd been great, that I didn't tell too many jokes and had got it just right. He flattered me rotten, asked me to do the warm-up for the next show too, and like a fool I said yes.

Then I asked him what I had said. He replied that he had no idea, but apparently it had gone down a bomb. So I went round all the crew asking them what I had said, because I had no idea either, and as whatever routine I had used had gone down so well I quite wanted to repeat it. I was lumbered with the warm-ups for Benny's shows ever after. I didn't miss one. But I never remembered what I said that very first time. The whole thing was just a haze. It led to me doing the warm-up for every light entertainment show Thames did for years – all because bloody Benny Hill and John Robins stuck me on without telling me what I was going to do. I even did warm-ups after I became a director myself.

I moved away from Benny for a time because I started my directing career with *The Epilogue*. It was the shortest programme on

TV, described by Michael Bentine as: 'Good Evening . . . click.' In those days every new director was given *The Epilogue* – a training ground unavailable today as we no longer have epilogues to close down TV stations at the end of the evening. And, come to think of it, TV rarely closes down at all.

Then I progressed to children's programmes like *Sooty* and *Rainbow*, and slowly came up through the ranks to variety. I didn't know at the time, but for three years running Benny asked for me to direct his show.

Phillip Jones, then head of Light Entertainment, asked me on his behalf every year and I always turned it down. I did so because Benny was already my friend, and also because I knew what hard work he was in those days. He had a reputation for being extremely difficult, and I thought our friendship would make it impossible.

In the end I gave in, because they kept forcing money into my hand. To begin with I thought I had made a mistake – that my original reaction, that Benny and I would not be able to work together as director and star, had been the right one. It was ironic the way things turned out, because we became such a good, strong team. It certainly didn't look at first as if that was going to happen.

Benny was a very big star, don't forget. And I was still a new director. On the first show I directed for him he was very naughty. There is no doubt in my mind that he was trying to test me. He pushed me to the limit to see if I would crack. Nothing was right. And he was out of order. He was finding fault quite unnecessarily.

On the first show we had a sequence in a bar and he didn't like it at all. It may be that he was unhappy with the whole strength of the material, but he just tore the practical side of it to pieces. Nothing was right. At the best of times Benny was always a perfectionist, which you couldn't quarrel with because that is what made him so good. And he was pedantic about costumes, sets and props. A lot of other comedians would say: 'That's near enough. That's fine. That'll do. That's funny enough.' But for Benny, no table ever fell over just as he wanted it to, at exactly the right time or in exactly the right crash order. And he would go on and on and on until it was right. But this particular day I soon realized it was never going to be right, whatever we did.

Ben had on a white suit against a silvery-coloured bar, and he reckoned that was wrong. So I said: 'OK, we'll change the colour of one or the other. Now let's move on to the gag with the table.' The table wasn't right, of course. The chair wasn't right. It was getting pretty predictable.

You couldn't really argue with him because he was fairly close to being correct, but he knew very well that a lot of what he was doing was not necessary. Finally he pointed to yet another set for yet another gag and he said: 'Oh dear, Oh dear. That's wrong.'

I thought to myself: 'Hang on, now hang about. This could go on for ever. This will go on for ever. I have to make a stand.'

So I broke the studio and I sat Benny down in the corner of the bar, and I said to him: 'I tell you what I am going to do, Ben. I'm going to break the whole studio for the day. Nothing here is going to be right with you today, nothing at all. So I'm not going to waste my time, nor any of these people's time. I'll go up to the boss and I'll organize you another day of studio time, and then you and I will sit down here together and we'll go through everything and we'll say that's wrong, that's wrong and that's wrong, and I'll have it all changed by the next time you come into the studio.'

Now studio time like that costs a fortune. To break that studio and send all those people home would have meant an incredible waste of money. Also, in those days there was so much going on at Thames that studio time was booked months ahead, so as soon as we were finished Drama or somebody else would be due to move in.

And remember, I was a young director with everything to prove. If I had been forced to break the studio the boss would have blamed me for not sorting out my own problems, and I could have been sacked. It would have been that serious.

Benny was shaken – which was entirely the intention. He knew all that. He knew everything about it. He said to me: 'You can't do it.'

I said: 'I can and I will, if I have to.'

He realized I wasn't kidding. Everything changed. He put his arm around me and said: 'Look, our Den. Surely we can work it out. If we had a blue tablecloth over there I think that table might be all right after all.'

And I said: 'Fine. OK. Let's try it with a blue tablecloth.'

Slowly we started working, and we ended up doing a ruddy good day's work. He began to call me 'Nature boy', which became his pet name for me; and, looking back, it was a good sign. Ben liked to call people by silly names – I think it may have been a kind of defence mechanism again, something vaguely amusing to hide behind. 'Little heart' and 'Little sausage' were standard for almost everyone. 'Nature boy' was all mine. I never knew quite why he chose that name, but I suppose it was because, as I am barely five foot eight tall and definitely not built like Tarzan, he liked the absurdity of it.

But 'Nature boy' or not, Benny had been testing me, really testing me. I knew it and I wasn't going to have it. I was prepared to put my head on the block, but I wasn't prepared to let him get away with that sort of behaviour, and once he understood that we really started to work as a team.

He was being deliberately, quite deliberately silly. And I just looked in those twinkly eyes of his and said to myself: 'You're not going to break me, sunshine. You're not going to do it.'

On that same show I learned a lesson about working with Benny that I never forgot. His opening number was the kind of slapstick routine that he always did brilliantly. It relied heavily on props. He was a cavalier coming home from the wars. His sword got jammed in a gate and the gate wouldn't open, and finally it opened the wrong way. Then he leaned on a table which collapsed and so on. We started to run through the sketch and I went up to the gallery to camera rehearse. Benny walked to the set, reached the gate and just stopped. He stood there looking at his nails, looking around. He was going no further.

I shouted: 'Hang on, I'm coming down.' Down the stairs I ran.

'What's the problem?' I asked him.

'It's the gate, Den.'

'Well, is it too high or too low, or what?'

'It's too high.'

'OK. We'll take six inches off it.' And up the stairs I ran.

'Action!' I called.

On he came. He got to the gate, looked at the gate, opened it. And then he stopped.

Down the stairs I trotted again.

'OK. What's the matter, Ben?'

'Do we have to have these steps, these two treads here?'

'Well, do you want to come straight on or do you want a ramp instead. What *do* you want?'

'I just didn't know there were going to be two steps, Den.'

'Look, you've got to come off the back rostrum. So, would you prefer a ramp? Or do you just want the steps lowered a bit?'

'I'll have the steps lowered.'

'OK. Designer, lower the steps a bit,' I called.

The job was done, and up those stairs to the gallery I trotted once more.

'Action!'

On Benny came. And yes. He stopped yet another time.

'I'm coming down,' I shouted and set off. At the top of the stairs it was my turn to stop and I thought to myself, 'What am I doing?'

I paused and chatted to a stagehand, and I had a word with the boom man, and I walked very slowly down those stairs – no running this time – aware that everyone was watching me and waiting.

Benny was watching and waiting too.

'Right,' I said. 'Let's go from the top, and let's walk through all the props minute by minute, shall we?'

We did that, and then when we started rolling I stayed on the studio floor with him. For the next sixteen years I never shot anything unless I was there with him on the studio floor, because the moment I went out of his eyeline he would stop. After that I never went up to the gallery until eight o'clock on the night that the studio audience was in, when I absolutely had to get off the studio floor.

Now that incident was not another test for me. He was not making trouble for the sake of it. It was all quite genuine. It was typical comic's insecurity. And the greater the comic, the greater the insecurity. Eric Morcambe used to say that humour was all based on fear. Comedians are always afraid, afraid they will lose their timing, afraid they won't get the laughs any more. Benny was no exception to that rule. He achieved a level of fame and fortune beyond his wildest dreams – but he never stopped being afraid.

FOUR

THE GLORY YEARS

Benny's years at Thames TV led to the most extraordinary international success, not only greater than that of any other comic but also exceeding the fame and fortune of almost any other entertainer. His shows sold to more than a hundred countries across the world and made him a multi-millionaire. No film star had a worldwide audience as great as Benny Hill's.

Thames TV International was set up almost entirely to handle overseas sales of Benny's shows. In 1984 the company won the Queen's Award for Export Achievement for selling programmes to 127 countries. This was high-powered stuff indeed – there are only 142 countries in the world with TV broadcasting facilities – and Benny's material made up the vast bulk of these sales. Just before his death his programmes were making five million dollars a year in overseas sales – money divided among Thames TV, the various agencies abroad and Benny himself, who had without doubt the best marketing deal in television. He picked up fifty per cent of profits on sales worldwide. At one point in 1990 *The Benny Hill Show* was actually on the schedule of ninety-seven TV channels throughout the world. Nobody in history has ever enjoyed that amount of syndication all at once. You could not get away from the man, wherever you went. He rode on the crest of a wave. He was a superstar and – make no mistake about it – Benny knew how big he was and he loved every moment of it.

At home in Britain his shows regularly topped the ratings, picking up audiences in excess of twenty million. He even used to beat *Coronation Street* to the number one slot – and in Britain that is no mean achievement. *The Street*, the world's longest-running soap, has only occasionally relinquished that number one spot in its incredible thirty-year-plus run.

Until he was sacked by Thames Benny had never really suffered even a minor setback in his TV career. He just rollercoasted from one triumph to another. America, in particular, fell at his feet, and he remains the only British comic in history to have conquered the States. He was always so sure-footed. It was Ben's own idea to produce a comedy feature film made up of clips from his Thames TV shows. He read in the American showbusiness paper *Variety* that Sid Caesar had taken ten sketches from his TV programme *Your Show of Shows* and put them together for the cinema.

'Oh, yes,' thought Ben. 'That's clever, and cheap too.'

Ben's project was backed by top impresario Bernard Delfont, and John Robins – Benny's first Thames TV director – was given the task of taking Ben's best TV material and editing it together to make a movie. The result, *The Best of Benny Hill*, was a ninety-minute feature film which cost £30,000 to make and raked in millions. It went on general release in Britain in 1974. Ben's American explosion was yet to happen.

New Yorker Don Taffner, boss of D. L. Taffner Ltd, marketed Thames's programmes in the States from the launch of Thames TV in 1968. At first he could not spark off interest in the idiosyncratic British comic called Benny Hill. American TV bosses complained that they could not understand Ben's humour and were baffled by his accent. They couldn't understand a word he said. Taffner countered that he couldn't understand a word Marlon Brando said, but it didn't stop Brando being a huge box office draw. Nobody was impressed.

But finally in 1978 the station WTAF in Philadelphia – not very big, not very rich, and struggling to survive – pronounced itself a prospective buyer. When the station manager, Ron Gold, was shown a tape of the show he was knocked out by Benny and immediately saw the potential. He pledged that WTAF would take all the *Benny Hill Shows* available. But there was a snag. Gold wanted the shows re-edited into a faster half-hour format which he felt would be more suitable for American TV. And that would be an expensive and risky process.

Taffner accepted that no way was Benny going to walk on to the huge and lucrative American network, but to make that kind of editing operation viable he had to find more buyers. It was imperative. He decided to put together a half-hour pilot, and after consulting Benny, his agent and the producers of his Thames show agreed that the best man for the job of masterminding the demo show aimed specifically for the American market would be John Street, Benny's director from his BBC days – now retired and living in Cornwall in the south-west of England.

John obediently abandoned his retirement and set to work. He concluded that it would take four British hours to make a slick American half-hour. Guest artists, jokes and routines that would only mean anything to British audiences had to go, and all of the rest of the material was ruthlessly cut and tightened up.

Taffner staged a convention in Los Angeles aimed at super-selling the new-look Benny Hill and at last managed to generate further interest. He struck no actual deals, but was confident enough to give John Street the go-ahead back in England to start compiling forty Benny half-hours. Ron Gold placed a formal order for all forty, and started showing Benny on the Philadelphia station as soon as the first three specially edited programmes arrived.

He began as he meant to go on, screening the shows five nights a week, and simply repeating them again and again in a regular 11 pm spot. The response was instant. WTAF's ratings began to climb steadily. It was autumn 1979. The warm glow of Benny's sunshine was about to rise across America.

TV bosses don't miss much over there. Within weeks there was a rush to get in on the Philadelphia act. TV companies all over the States placed orders for *The Benny Hill Show*. It became a cult. If you hadn't seen *The Benny Hill Show* you were suddenly a nobody. And strangely, from the very start Benny was trendy in America, which is something he probably never has been in England.

Bennymania happened with such speed and almost of its own volition – even Taffner and certainly Benny were astonished. Because he was not on network, but syndicated individually to stations across the country, Benny's shows were accompanied by no national publicity and very little advertising. They generated their own popularity which, by the early eighties, had reached hysterical proportions. In New York the *Daily News* recorded *The Benny Hill Show*'s success on WOR Channel Nine. 'The ratings have sky-rocketed, making it the highest rating show on the station. It also tops all the independents in the week-night 11pm period.'

Back in England, John Street and the Thames team were working overtime to keep up with the endless demand for more and more shows. Benny Hill T-shirts, posters and car stickers were marketed. A card was even produced to hang on doorknobs, warning: 'Do not disturb! We are watching Benny Hill.' And all this happened without the star himself. Benny steadfastly refused to visit America until 1984. It was all too much for him.

Meanwhile, his musical recording career also soared to heights unequalled by any other comic. Ben had begun to make records in the sixties for Pye. One of their producers was composer Tony Hatch, whose job it was to instrumentalize some of the songs Benny had first written for TV shows and turn them into slick modern records.

The first, in 1961, was 'Gather in the Mushrooms', a gently suggestive number about a young man going courting in the countryside. Its sales were instantly boosted when the BBC revealed it had considered banning the record because it was too naughty. Two more singles, 'Transistor Radio' and 'Harvest of Love', followed during the sixties and all three were Top Twenty hits. An album, *Benny Hill Sings*, was also a hit, as were several more singles. But none of this prepared Benny for the sensation caused in 1971 when, at the height of his powers, he released his biggest hit, 'Ernie: The Fastest Milkman in the West'.

It was based on his own days as a milkman, when Ben imagined himself Sheriff Wyatt Earp riding shotgun aboard the Wells Fargo stagecoach driving into Dodge City. Ben wrote the song as part of a sketch based on the TV talent contest show *Opportunity Knocks*. We filmed it with me off screen banging two pieces of wood together to make the noise of a whip cracking while Ben brandished his prop whip. The lyrics were simple and silly:

> He galloped into Market Street
> His badge upon his chest
> His name was Ernie
> And he drove the fastest milkcart in the West.

You can't help smiling at the daftness of it, and the record was an instant smash, hurtling to the number one spot in the charts. When Benny was invited on to *Top of the Pops*, the very thought terrified him. He compromised by making a short film for the BBC, featuring him dressed as a milkman and driving a horse and milkcart, which could accompany his smash hit recording.

There were not many areas of showbusiness that Benny Hill failed to conquer. I think he would have rather liked to star in his own Hollywood movie, but he never wanted to devote the time necessary to a project like that and he certainly never wanted to live in the States, much as he grew to love visiting there. He liked to travel, but he knew where his home was.

He was always getting offers to play Las Vegas or Atlantic City, and he was told he could name his price. But Benny hated performing live and didn't want to know. He turned down the TV chat shows as he did in Britain, and this led to some confusion in the States. As he became more and more successful in America and the demand grew for more of his work, so the shows which were transmitted became older and older as Thames dug into its film library to unearth yet another offering for the eager American market. And because he never appeared on *Carson* or similar shows – which was second nature to all big American stars – a lot of Americans thought he was dead when he first began to appear on their screens in the mid-seventies. While he was at the peak of his popularity everywhere and on top of the world, we used to get a lot of letters asking if he was still alive.

His fan mail was extraordinary. He received hundreds of letters and parcels every week, and everything that came to him personally he would handle. Of course the bulk of the stuff used to go to Thames and they dealt with a lot of it, but the rest of it Benny did himself. And he was meticulous about it: every reply was handwritten by Benny. I never understood why he did not employ a secretary, but that was typical of Ben. 'Oh no, little heart. I don't want a secretary telling me what to do and sorting me out. I'll do it my way, thank you very much.' Typical of Benny's attitude to everything, really.

Most of the letters were average fan correspondence asking for photographs and autographs – that sort of thing. It used to annoy him hugely when people asked for a photograph and didn't send a stamped addressed envelope. He thought that was a cheek, but the pictures were always sent. He tried to avoid writing proper letters to people, because when he did that he automatically became their best friend and the correspondence would go on for ever. If then he tried to break it off by not answering the last letter, that would make him seem rude and arrogant. Benny also got his share of declarations of undying love and proposals of marriage, and that had to be handled with great delicacy.

So it was a dangerous game that he chose to play all alone in his little Teddington flat. As well as being tiresome, dealing with fan mail is not easy, which is why most celebrities employ somebody to walk through the minefield for them. But Benny preferred to take on the burden himself. He accepted it as part of the job, and would shut himself away for days on end to get through whole batches of it.

He also used to be sent gifts from all over the world. There was one lady in America who used to send him tea, presumably on the basis that he was English so he must love the stuff. Several time a year she sent him decorative parcels, and he used to come round to my house clutching armfuls of them, saying: 'Which would you like? I've got Earl Grey, Darjeeling, Assam, several kinds of herb tea. I've got it all. Can I interest you in a nice cuppa?' In fact he used to give a lot of presents away. He'd arrive at the studio, for instance, with a cuddly toy for my daughter Joanna and thirty-seven Swiss chocolate bars which he would distribute among the girls. He never sent gifts back, because that would hurt people. A lot of things went to charities like Mencap, and flowers and plants would go to hospitals.

I don't think Benny was ever sent anything that he felt he couldn't keep, like a gold watch. And I don't think he was ever sent anything saucy either, like a pair of knickers or a suspender belt. Although his humour was naughty, Ben was never going to be regarded as a sex symbol – much as he might secretly have liked to have been – so his mail was pretty clean. Women fans wanted to cuddle him and even to marry him, but they didn't even consider seducing him. Poor old Ben.

And, famous as he was and as he knew he was, if people called after him in the street he would never look round unless they said his name. He always felt that it couldn't be him they were shouting to. And he dreaded turning round and waving only to discover that whoever it was had actually been trying to attract the attention of their brother across the road, and had not even noticed Benny. He could be very easily embarrassed – and that situation would have embarrassed him.

Meanwhile, as the biggest comedy star in the world was modestly skulking around the streets of London and Southampton, where he had been brought up, the demand for him worldwide reached staggering proportions. He became loved not only in the Western world but throughout the then Eastern bloc. In China he became the greatest hero since Mao Tse-tung. And, who knows, perhaps it was really Benny and not Gorbachev who brought glasnost to the Soviet Union.

The Russians discovered Benny before he was even allowed on the air in their country by tuning their TV aerials towards Finland to pick up Western TV shows. On New Years' Eve 1989 he made his official debut with a fifteen-minute introductory special which he began by greeting the people in Russian. '*Chactaliviy e prazdnichney 1989*,' he said. 'Happy and festive 1989.' It became routine for Benny to launch all his shows abroad with a few specially recorded words in the native language.

The staggering success of his programmes led to Benny constantly being asked to make TV commercials across the globe. In Australia he advertised a department store called Walton's, which sold everything from underwear to hardware. In Greece in 1983 he was paid £25,000 for a day's work making a TV commercial for German Kaiser beers. In Spain he was hired to promote a make of TV set called SABA, appearing first as a German, then as an Englishman, then as an Italian and finally as a Japanese viewer, all explaining why SABA was the best TV in the world. Longest-running and best-known of all were his French TV commercials for Jacques Brunch biscuits. These went on for years, and even in the early eighties Ben was paid £80,000 for ten thirty-second ads.

It was all lucrative, high-profile stuff, and Benny knew it. Asked in 1982 why he was still refusing to visit America even though he was already a folk hero there, Ben replied: 'I'll go if they find me something small, exciting and easy – and I don't mean a blonde. I thought perhaps a TV commercial.' Maybe Ron Rice, the boss of the Hawaiian Tropic sun tan lotion company, heard him, because a few years later Ben was signed up to promote their products in the United States and judge their beauty competitions in the Bahamas and Florida.

Throughout it all, his home-produced *Benny Hill Show* remained the most important part of Ben's life. That was his professional power base. It was all his. He lived and breathed it. It represented the culmination of his every dream.

His attention to detail was absolute. Even those who did not approve of his material could never fault Ben's use of it. And he never stopped until it was perfect. Once in our early days together he made eighty cuts in a seven-minute sketch. I was horrified. I said he was a butcher. He told me that wasn't true. He was cutting with meticulous care, and each cut was only one and a half seconds. I queried whether in that case it was worth doing. 'Eighty one and a half seconds add up to two minutes, and of course it's worth doing,' said Ben. 'Cut a dull two minutes from a seven-minute sketch and you end up with a five-minute sketch that's like a flash of lightning. Very fast, very sharp, and very, very, bright!'

During all those glory years Benny's show was frequently nominated for awards all over the world. He received awards for his records, too. He picked up a gold disc for his recording of 'Ernie'. There can't be too many comics with a gold disc stashed away.

In the eighties his recording career took off in America also. One day I was in the office of a friend of mine, Adrian Hilliard, who ran a production company called Hunky Dory. He showed me a fax he had just received from an American record producer called Nick Cowan, who was looking for a new British recording artist. All the top names, like Phil Collins and Elton John, were signed up with big labels and Cowan wanted someone original.

I suggested doing an LP of Benny's comedy songs for the American market, and Cowan telephoned to say he loved the idea. Benny never looked back. We just took songs from his various shows and recorded them. It was easy because Benny always wrote his own words and music, so he owned the copyright of all his songs. And his records ended up about as popular worldwide as his TV shows.

In 1988 he made a rock video with Genesis, probably the biggest rock band in the world, to promote their latest record

'Anything She Does', which was about topless models. Benny was hired to add some humour. Genesis' Phil Collins, a huge superstar, astonishingly pronounced himself in awe of Benny. 'He's one of my heroes,' he said.

Benny was moved, as he always was when major showbusiness stars paid tribute to him. After all, these were the people who understood how tough it could be at the top. Tributes and awards continued to roll in during the eighties. Ben won the comedy award at the prestigious Montreux TV Festival – a great honour in television – and he was very proud of that. But I have no doubt that to Benny the greatest accolade of all was when he was presented with the Chaplin Award for Comedy.

There have only ever been a handful of these awards, and Charlie Chaplin, of course, was Benny's great idol. We were invited by the Chaplin Foundation to fly to Vevey in Switzerland for their annual comedy film festival. Benny was the honorary president of the jury, a role which he only agreed to take on after it was clarified that he would not have to do any judging himself, because he so disliked criticizing the work of other artists.

Eugene Chaplin, Charlie's son, was there, and one lunchtime he took us to his father's house where we walked round the grounds and had lunch by the pool. After lunch he took us into the house to his father's sitting room and his father's study, where Benny, thrilled to bits, was invited to sit in Charlie Chaplin's chair. He was in heaven.

Then Eugene took us to a little room with a TV set and a video recorder and showed us a row of videotapes on a shelf. They were all of Benny Hill shows.

'My father used to sit here and watch you all the time. He thought you were the greatest,' Eugene told Benny.

I had never seen Benny quite so overwhelmed. He could not believe what he was seeing and hearing. There were tears in his eyes.

But the ultimate honour was still to come. On the last night of the festival the crowds gathered in the town square of Vevey for an open air closing ceremony, and it was then that this beautiful Chaplin Award for his contribution to comedy was presented to Benny. It was a highly polished, slightly abstract bronze of *The Little Tramp*, about eighteen inches high, and apart from what it represents it is a stunning trophy in its own right.

The crowd clapped and cheered and roared its approval and then Benny walked off the stage, came up to me, plonked the award in my hands said said: 'There you are, our Den. You deserve this as much as I do.'

There were tears in my eyes then. I shall remember that moment as long as I live.

FIVE

HOME COMFORTS

None of that glory, no achievement, no amount of money was ever going to change Benny Hill. He lived in a modest rented flat in Teddington, Middlesex, just up the road from Thames TV Studios. It was an anonymous, soul-less place. A bit like a room in your average American motel, but not quite so luxurious.

Benny owned hardly anything in it. He rented the place fully furnished. Not even the crockery in the kitchen belonged to him. The pictures on the wall were of the harmless variety bought by the crate by professional decorators working on a limited budget. Benny had no collection of framed paintings or prints of his own, no family photographs, no ornaments or knick-knacks of any kind collected on his travels. The flat was totally without personal touches.

It was probably the only home I have been in which gave virtually no clues to who lived there. Guests on the Lloyd Grossman/David Frost TV show *Through the Keyhole* are shown film clips of homes of the famous and asked to guess the occupants. They would have had no chance with Benny's pad. About all you learned from the place was that whoever lived there loved TV and couldn't care less about his surroundings. Benny's only personal possessions at Teddington were a small collection of videotapes, two television sets and three video recorders – one for the American system – in his living room. And they were all lined up on the floor in front of his sofa.

The place was always slightly grubby and very untidy. There was usually a pile of dirty dishes in the kitchen. The living room table was permanently covered with piles of papers: newspapers, letters, envelopes containing scripts, chocolate wrappings and goodness knows what else covered in scribbled notes.

More of this debris was probably to be found on the floor in front of his favourite sofa. There were also stacks of photographs. He used to like to have the stills photographs from his shows, particularly of him and any of the girls of course, and pictures from our trips abroad. But they just lay around in dusty piles. The only picture I can ever remember him having framed was a photograph of him taken a long time ago after a *Royal Variety Show* with the Queen and the Duke of Edinburgh. He must have been very proud of it. But it was not hung anywhere that I know of for many years.

The bathroom had a slightly unsavoury air about it. And Benny never made his bed. On the very rare occasions when he invited visitors back to his flat he was always running about closing doors to hide the worst of the mess – particularly the permanently unmade bed which seemed to embarrass him. The obvious remedy, to make it every morning, was beyond him.

I am afraid my mate Ben was a slob at home. When he was alone he just did not notice the mess around him, and the way he kept house was undoubtedly one of the reasons why he could only live alone and was so pathologically opposed to visits. Without doubt I was Benny's closest friend, but even I was only occasionally invited to Fairwater House.

He had a cleaning lady, Lynne, who did her best to clear up once a fortnight. But she was only barely tolerated by Benny. He didn't really like people invading his territory. And she was under strict instructions not to move anything. So she had to dust and hoover painstakingly around the debris. He would even cover up piles of paper with sheets so that she would not disturb them. She usually changed the sheets on the bed, and that was the only time the bed ever got properly made up. The flat was then super-clean for a bit, not least because Benny had always spent at least two days fussing and trying rather unsuccessfully to clear up before she was due. That, of course, was another reason he did not like having a cleaning lady.

He really was a scruff. He had the ability to wreck a hotel room in minutes. We would be away on a trip and he would maybe just have a briefcase with him containing one change of clothes. His papers, his pills for headaches and for his ulcer, a shirt, a spare pair of underpants and a spare pair of socks and nothing more – all in one briefcase.

Yet I would go to his room a couple of hours later and it would be a wreck. There would be newspapers everywhere. Bits of *TV Times* over here. Toothbrush over there. Comb somewhere else. Shirt on the floor. Chaos. You would smack a kid for keeping a room like that. Sometimes I suggested we sort things out. Not a popular move. 'Shall I tidy up a bit, Ben? This is disgusting.'

'Don't you dare! Don't touch anything!' he then yelled. He was like W. C. Fields in that film where he is a clerk who keeps all his papers jumbled in a bureau but is proved, none the less, to be indispensable. Ben knew where everything was. Or he thought he did. We had a gag about it. I said: 'Why do you throw all your clothes on the floor?'

'Because they won't stick to the ceiling,' he replied.

His philosophy about the way he lived was simple. He explained it like this: 'I think to myself, "Shall I go to the cinema this afternoon, or shall I clean up the flat because it's a tip?" So I ask myself what will happen if I leave it looking a tip and go to the cinema. The answer is nothing. So I go to the cinema.' Infallible logic. That was Ben. You see, none of that kind of stuff meant anything to him. He was a man who needed so little.

The nearest he ever got to a proper home was his flat in Queens Gate, West London, where he lived for twenty years. But even that was odd. He had a bedroom, a small dining room at the back and a lovely great big living room that he never went into. It was like when you were a little kid years ago and the front room was reserved for visitors.

I remember being escorted into this room the first time I went to that flat, and you could tell nobody ever went into it – that it wasn't lived in at all. 'When did you last come in here?' I asked him.

'I don't know – six months ago,' he replied. And to him there was nothing remotely strange about that. Before someone was coming he used to go into the front room and turn the heating on, and maybe open the windows to air it.

He existed entirely in his little dining room where he had put a tiny sofa and his drinks cabinet, and he had his television and telephone on a coffee table in front of him. That was all he wanted. He was either sitting there writing on that table or watching TV or on the telephone. If not, he was in the kitchen, in bed or in the bath. What did he need that other, bigger, grander room for?

The TV Times once decorated that big front room for an article and put new furniture in. They did it in style – there were rows of ornaments supplied, pictures, everything. Then all the current Hill's Angels arrived and were photographed with him for the magazine: Benny Hill at home with his girls. When the photo session was over Benny told the girls to take anything they wanted. He didn't want the ornaments or the pictures on the wall. He didn't want any of it really. He just shut the door on that beautiful redecorated room and went back to living the way he was before – in front of his coffee table in the little room at the back.

I thought it was crazy. Then one day I noticed that he still had a black and white TV. I hadn't realized, because he didn't usually have the set on when I was there. For me it was just the final straw. 'What's the matter with you?' I asked. 'Why on earth haven't you got a colour telly?'

He looked at me in amazement. It honestly had not crossed his mind. 'OK,' he said, and he obediently sought out the Yellow Pages, picked up the phone and ordered himself a new telly. On the spot. When the delivery man arrived with it I was there, and I sneakily arranged for him to put the set in the big, grand, newly decorated front room.

That ploy worked a treat – for a while. Benny actually started to use the big room and live halfways properly. But then the new TV broke down. It just had to, didn't it? He did nothing about getting the set repaired. He just moved back to his old ways, his little old room and the black and white set on the coffee table.

Eventually I made arrangements for the colour TV to be fixed – well, Benny wasn't going to do it, was he? – but when it came back that ended up in the cluttered little room as well. I had tried. Ben had his way as usual. I gave up. What could you do with the man?

He moved out of Queens Gate because of building work to extend the block in which he lived. The project was expected to take years to complete, and the noise and the dust were driving Benny mad. He always loved to sit outside, and he could not use his balcony because of the mess. Finally, after two years of it and no end in sight, even Benny had endured enough.

My wife Mary found him the Teddington flat. He put all his furniture in storage, and the idea was that he would look for a house to buy. Mary was called in to find properties for him to have a look at, but I don't think he was ever serious. He wasn't even sure about moving out into the suburbs at first, but he grew to love Teddington. He particularly enjoyed living by the Thames and being able to go for long walks along the river bank to Richmond and Kingston. Being Ben, he did not need more than three rooms. He had those in the rented flat, and that was quite enough.

He would frequently wander off on long, aimless riverside walks, saying that he had been having a peep at properties he knew were for sale, because he liked to study the outside alone before disturbing the people who lived there. If he didn't like the outside he would not want to go in and didn't need to bother anyone.

When he and Mary went house-hunting they used to look for places in the morning and then Ben would take Mary for a lavish lunch. As ever, he loved lunching with ladies, and I was fairly convinced that the true purpose of these expeditions for Benny was a nice morning out followed by a good lunch and a good bottle of wine. There was always something wrong with the properties he looked at. There was one lovely house overlooking Richmond Park which even he fell for. He went back to look at it two or three times, but he was worried because there was an empty church right next door. 'You never know what they might do to it, little heart,' he said. 'They might turn it into a disco or something.' It was only later that it occurred to me that Benny was in the position to buy the empty church as well, just as insurance, if he really wanted to.

The furniture storage cost him a small fortune, of course, but it didn't bother him. I think it was a relief to him not to have to be worried with all those nasty material things. I used to tell him off for wasting thousands of pounds a year on storing furniture, which, quite frankly, was not worth a great deal. 'Oh, little heart,' he would say. 'It will all have a place when I find a house of my own.'

I told him he ought to scrap the lot and buy new. No chance.

'Ah, but there's a nice record player there,' he said.

'A record player. And how old is that?' I asked him. 'Everybody else in the world has a sophisticated sound system, but you have a record player and that's in storage. Has it got wooden needles?'

'No, Dennis. It hasn't got wooden needles.' He could play straight man very well when he wanted to. And he always called me Dennis when he was being stroppy or just didn't want to continue with a discussion.

It simply did not enter his head to go out and buy a modern system with tapes and discs and all of that. It wasn't meanness – it really wasn't. He just didn't care. Once when I'd had a real go at him he started to ask me about my music system and how much it cost, which was about £400. 'Oh I must get one of those, then,' he said. But he never did.

He had an old radio, which he kept in the loo. A tatty, ancient piece of machinery. And he had a tape recorder which was even older. But they both worked perfectly, so what was the point in replacing them? That was the way Ben's mind worked.

He had no books, not even in storage. I can't remember Benny reading a book. I can never remember him saying, 'Hey, I'm halfway through the new John Le Carré novel,' or anything like that. He enjoyed cartoon books because they gave him ideas for sketches. That was Benny, always plotting. Always working.

Apart from the TVs and video recorders and tapes, his only other possessions were clothes. He had several beautiful suits but he totally misused them. He would wear the brown jacket with the grey trousers and look a total mess. Ben had funny feet, very broad and awkward with high insteps like Tommy Cooper, so if he found a pair of shoes which were comfortable and fitted him he would wear them for ever, until they were falling off his feet. You can see that on recordings of his shows if you look carefully. Whatever else he may be wearing, you can spot the same brown shoes again and again. He had cupboards full of shirts because he liked to travel very light and hated packing to go away. So he was inclined to travel with little more than he was wearing and just buy himself a couple of new shirts rather than carry them with him.

When we were working away from home, doing picture calls or something like that, I used to get together with our lovely mate Brian at Thames wardrobe and we would sort out a nice jacket, trousers, shirts – the lot – out of the Benny Hill TV wardrobe. Brian and I would pack his blessed case for him and he would just open it up and there would be complete outfits down to ties, handkerchiefs, belts – even a hat if called for. Benny loved that. Perfect for him. He didn't even have to do his own packing.

He didn't own a car, and never drove one. He had been a driver – a most reluctant one – in the army during the World War II when he had had to drive thousands of miles. He told me that when he left the army he decided he would never get behind the wheel again unless it was absolutely necessary. At first, of course, he couldn't even afford a car, and later on he reckoned that being without one would encourage him to walk, which he thoroughly enjoyed and which he always hoped – in vain, I think – would reduce his pudding tummy.

For longer distances he liked to be driven, and one of his extravagances was to hire a chauffeur-driven car at the drop of a hat. Benny would happily spend a great deal of money on the few things that mattered to him. The best hotels. The best restaurants. And the best and most comfortable way of travelling.

He always flew first-class, of course. And when he hired a car it was usually a limo, with the kind of driver who knew how to look after his clients. He would hire a car to take him any distance rather than go by train, which he didn't really like – he was too vulnerable, too famous, and people would crowd around him. So he would hire a limo to drive the length and breadth of the country if necessary.

He also hired cars to take him to the laundry. Naturally he did not own a washing machine, and if he had owned one he would never have got round to using it. Instead he took his washing to a local laundry, where it was all done for him. At one time he used to walk there quite happily if the load wasn't too big. But after all the stuff in the papers about him carrying his belongings around in tatty carrier bags he became a little sensitive about his image. A bit late, if you ask me.

Anyway, he drew the line at walking to the laundry carrying his smalls. When possible he dropped off his washing when he was being picked up by a hire car to go on a longer journey of some kind. But every so often he did actually hire a chauffeur-driven car just to take him to the laundry.

Something I realize that I miss dreadfully is the way Benny and I would set off on our travels together. It was stylish and brought a bit of luxury into my life, but it was also very funny. He always came to pick me up, because I lived closer to the airport than he did. He arrived in some lovely hired limo with a driver, and as it was almost always early in the morning when we flew it became a regular occurrence that Ben would pick up a bottle of milk off the doorstep, ring the bell and then hand me the milk – a throw-back to his milkman days. Then we would burst into an impromptu rendering of his hit song 'Ernie: The Fastest Milkman in the West'. 'Ernie! Ernie!' we would cry, really giving it everything. The neighbours loved us – although they didn't complain. Benny Hill could get away with murder. All daft, really – but God, do I miss it.

There's something else he did which I keep thinking about now that he's dead: he always picked up my suitcase and carried it to the car. Every time. I took it for granted because it was just part of our routine, but it was a lovely touch. And I miss the scenes at the airport where passengers of all nationalities would besiege Ben. I used to be part of that, and I admit I loved it.

Ben also used chauffeur-driven cars to take him to his house in Southampton. The three-bedroomed semi with bay windows had been the family home, and he kept it simply because it was his mother's dying wish that he should never sell it. He didn't want a second home. That was nonsense to Ben. You can only live in one house at a time, can't you?

At first, I know, he would much rather have been without the house – he went down there only out of a sense of duty, to make sure that it wasn't falling apart and that somebody was mowing the lawn and all of that. But in recent years he had rediscovered Southampton, taking off in between work and spending a couple of weeks there several times a year. He used to wander round the docks, go off into the New Forest for long rambles, and take the ferry over to the Isle of Wight. He even had the house completely redecorated and re-plumbed, which was really going over the top for Ben. Roger Whatling, husband of Ben's great friend and former Hill's Angel, Sue Upton, is a builder, so he went down there for a couple of weeks and did the lot.

It was still somebody's house, though. The furniture and everything in the place remained just the way they were when his mother died. I don't think Ben changed anything. He just had no interest. His flat and the house in Southampton were just bases for him where he kept the few things he couldn't live without and where he could watch television as much as he liked.

But he did not endlessly shut himself away from the outside world. He was no hermit, no recluse. The reclusive sad clown label was another great myth, and Ben hated it. The papers made a meal of it, and you can see why – it's such a nice easy line. But it wasn't the truth about Benny Hill. He was more complicated than that.

Ben could be reclusive. He liked his own home and his own company, and he liked to be able to disappear into his own little world at will. But he could also be totally gregarious. It depended on his mood. He loved parties – though not big public showbiz bashes, first nights, Variety Club lunches and that sort of thing. No, that wasn't Benny. And in fact he turned down repeated invitations to join the Variety Club and the Water Rats, although he would always buy a table for their celebrity lunches and dinners and give the tickets away. He was quite happy to support the charity as long as he didn't have to go to the do himself. But he loved parties with his friends, wining and dining with his mates.

And I have fond if hazy memories of the way we used to celebrate his birthday. It was on 21 January and always fell in the middle of rehearsals for *The Benny Hill Show*. I knew well in advance not to plan any work at all for that day. It was the most important date in the world to Ben, and it didn't matter if we were behind schedule or had other problems with the show, on 21 January, the world stopped.

Benny used to throw a real shindig. He always insisted on having the entire cast and crew there, and if anything got in the way there was hell to pay. He fretted for days before. He hired an entire restaurant, and chose the menu and worked out the seating plan himself. It seemed like he put as much thought into arranging his birthday party as he did into an entire hour-long special. Like the shows, the party had to be perfect. Everybody had to be sitting next to the right person to make it swing. He had to have the right girl on either side of him. But nobody must be offended or feel left out, and so on . . . .

The restaurant was usually the nearest one to wherever our rehearsal rooms happened to be, and he always paid in readies, never wrote a cheque. It was an amazing day – every time. There would be wine and champagne coming out of our ears by the end of it. And the bill must always have been so enormous, that come to think of it, Uncle Ben probably could have done with one of those famous supermarket plastic bags in which to carry all the necessary cash. There was certainly nothing shy or retiring about Benny Hill on those occasions that I recall.

'Did you see that story this morning about me being so sad and lonely and reclusive?' he once telephoned me to say. 'They should have seen me in the South of France last week being reclusive with those six girls.'

His version was probably not quite the truth either, but it was natural with him to try to turn everything into a gag.

And locally, around Teddington and Southampton, he lived what was probably a very normal life – so normal that it would be viewed as eccentric because he was Benny Hill, superstar. Of course Benny did his own shopping. He liked shopping, and, anyway, who else was going to do it? Benny with a live-in housekeeper? Forget it. He would rather have slept rough in his own cardboard box than shared his funny little flat with anyone else.

On his way back from the shops in Teddington he would often stop off at our favourite boozer, the King's Head, and sit outside with a beer and a sandwich reading the newspapers. People came to take him for granted and he was not bothered much, which he liked. But he would wave to passers by, and if anyone approached him he was quite prepared to sign the odd autograph. Still more unreclusive behaviour.

He quite often walked to Kingston or Richmond and spent the afternoon in a cinema watching a film. He loved movies – a passion dating back to his schooldays – and was quite happy to sit and watch them surrounded by people. In fact I think he believed that to get the best from a film you should see it in the cinema and not on the video machine at home. It was not just the wide screen that attracted. That dark secret world, silently shared with an anonymous audience, suited him. He was certainly not interested in movie premieres.

His favourite sport was perhaps not one you would instantly associate with Ben, although there has always been quite a showbiz link. Like a lot of artists, he adored boxing and loved to attend big matches. Once we went to a boxing match in New York together, and because Benny is so huge in America he became more of an attraction than the fight. I realized that all the cameras around the ring were pointing at Ben and not at the boxers.

'Hope nobody gets knocked out, or these snappers will be in trouble,' I said to Ben.

He began to ham it up then, of course. He was always quick to slip into an act. Well, after all, what could be better than a Fred Scuttle salute to hide behind? Once Benny was safely into character – almost any character – he was comfortable. Then he could talk freely and give away absolutely nothing about himself. Which was invariably the intention.

SIX

WOMEN AND BENNY

Benny Hill never married. During the time I knew him there was never one serious girlfriend. And there was always an air of mystery about his life which led to constant speculation about his sexuality. But I can dismiss for all time any suggestion that Benny was gay. He was not homosexual. He was as straight as could be. He loved women. And over the years he slept with a lot of women.

He was not as sexually successful as he would have liked to be for three reasons. First, baby-faced and plump, he was no woman's idea of a sex object. They wanted to mother him and maybe give him a cuddle and laugh at his jokes, but they didn't very often want to sleep with him. Second, as he became more and more famous he became increasingly afraid of lurid kiss-and-tell stories in the more sensational Sunday papers. He would only ever go with women he knew well and trusted. He was really afraid of taking somebody home with him and then at the weekend reading all about what he was supposed to have done – or not done, as the case may be.

He was terribly upset when the *News of the World* carried a kiss-

and-tell from a former Page Three girl called Stefanie Marrian under the headline: 'Benny Made Me His Sex Slave'. She claimed that she contacted him as an 'innocent sixteen-year-old' trying to break into showbusiness.

And in the article, carried in October 1985, Stefanie claimed:

I was star-struck when we met. I asked him how to become an actress.
He invited me to his flat for an 'audition' – and produced a bottle of
*   champagne to help me relax. Benny told me there were three ways*
*   of becoming a success.*
Either you need talent which you don't have, or outstanding beauty
*   which you don't have either. Or you scratch my back, and I'll*
*   scratch yours.*

Stefanie then said that this was the start of a bizarre one-sided sexual relationship, which she described as 'demeaning', which lasted six years. She carried on seeing him because she believed it would further her career. 'I was dreaming of a speaking part he might give me,' she explained. For six years, Stef?

'I suppose it must be hard to understand,' she admitted. She was dead right. And any grudge she felt she had against Ben had been harboured for a long time. Stefanie was thirty-five when she decided to kiss and tell. The first sexual encounter with Ben which she so vividly described – 'He took me through to his bedroom, undressed me, and then stripped to his underpants. He looked like a white whale' – was allegedly nineteen years previously.

Poor Ben – he was mortified. 'It's so unfair,' he lamented. 'She has been allowed to tell it in her way, but I haven't been able to give my side. It wasn't the way she made it sound at all.'

Several other girls tried to get in on the act, including former Hill's Angel Nikki Critcher with whom Benny never had any kind of affair. But she claimed that once, in the studio, he had grabbed her breasts so hard that she had to slap his face to make him let go. I always found that hard to accept. Benny was not someone who

Top: Ben as Detective Lacey –
played by Tyne Daly – from the TV
series *Cagney & Lacey*.

Above. Henry McGee with Ben as
Fred Scuttle.

Right. 'Suzy, this is another fine
mess you've got me in.' Benny and
Sue Upton as Laurel and Hardy.
(*Scope Features*)

Previous page. The Hill family.
Benny, aged 13; his father, Alfred;
his sister, Diana; his mother, Helen
and his brother, Leonard. (*Sunday
Mirror*)

Top. Ben, the ladies man, in his element with two of his Hill's Angels. Diana Darvey, on his left, also sang with Ben.

Above. Boatman, Henry McGee is asking for an 'oar'. Ben brings him the wrong kind, played by Louise English.

Left. Fireman Ben doesn't know who to rescue – with the first Hill's Angel, Sue Bond. *(Scope Features)*

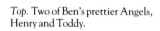

Top. Two of Ben's prettier Angels, Henry and Toddy.

Above. Henry's the Angel this time. Sue Upton ages suddenly. (*Scope Features*)

Above. Jon Jon Keefe upstages the just visible Benny – the team at work.

Left. Not The Bachelors – The Spatulas – Henry, Ben and Jackie Wright, the oldest and baldest of the stooges. (*Scope Features*)

Top. Ben at war. It's actually the team on location – much the same thing.

Above. Which one is the prisoner? Kirkland and Hill.

Left. OK. So you didn't like the shot . . . . (*Scope Features*)

Top. Ben and Charles Aznavour, two guys who know their onions.

Above. Ben pretends to write for the camera outside Paris's famous writers' café, Les Deux Magots. (*Barry Brecken*)

Above. Me making a spectacle of myself with Ben in Paris. (*Barry Brecken*)

Left. Only at Gatwick and I'm bored already.

Far left. Triple Scuttle. Three Freds on a bed which once belonged to Napoleon's daughter. Salutes from the British Ambassador, Sir Ewen Fergusson. his wife and Ben.

Above. Look what we found in the bath. Ben and I with Britt Ekland.

Right. No wonder Ben looks so happy. Four beauty queens and not a Kirkland in sight. *(Barry Brecken)*

touched other people much, and he was the last man in the world to do that to a woman. He always had too much respect for them. No wonder he became afraid to take women home with him if he could be accused of that sort of thing in public.

That was all nasty stuff, but the third reason why Benny did not have many successful sexual encounters with women was the most important. He was afraid of good sexual relationships because of what they might lead to. Benny was fiercely independent and lived life in a way which, while it appeared perfectly normal to him, seemed thoroughly peculiar to most people. Any woman Benny might become involved with would have to fit into that lifestyle and cope with the days of dieting, the eating binges, every night spent in front of the television and the constant obsession with work. Benny was not prepared to take the risk of becoming close to someone who might try to change him or anything about him. So, more often that not, he did not become involved.

He was not a lonely man, but he was a loner. And I think he felt that he was better off on his own. He always liked to live alone. And once he could afford to be independent he never moved in with a girl or even shared a flat with another bloke. The only time he ever lived in close daily contact with other people after leaving his parents' home in Southampton was when he was in the army and in his early days as a touring comic. He once lived in a hostel in East London, he stayed in various showbiz digs, and right after the war he did live in a flat-share in London. But none of that was out of choice. Benny always needed to know that he could retreat into his own space and shut his own front door on the world.

He became the total confirmed bachelor, but he was offended and astonished that this should lead to speculation that he was homosexual. And in 1982 he was moved to the point of publicity defending his sexuality, out of character for Ben, in an interview with the *Daily Mirror*'s Clifford Davis.

'I know all about the rumours and what people say about me,' he said.

'But from what I've seen of married life, it doesn't seem all that attractive. Only about a third of today's marriages seem to me to be happy. The other two-thirds either end up in divorce or the husband and wife are only staying together because of the children.

'Some people think that because I'm not married there's something strange about me.

'But I'm not gay, and I'm no weirdo.

'Of course I have occasional affairs with girls. But I'm always very discreet.'

Benny told me how, when he first started working in showbiz and was in a show with a group of gay dancers, one of them asked him if he was queer. But the seventeen-year-old Benny Hill did not even know what he meant. He remembered causing great confusion first of all by saying that he felt quite well, and then, when pressed, muttering something like: 'Not really, but I've got my funny little ways.'

Not long after that, Benny gained his one and only experience of the gay casting couch. The major partner of a well-known double act at the time needed a new sidekick and auditioned young Ben – at his flat with lashings of booze. Ben, unused to alcohol, was quickly under the influence and it was some time before he fully appreciated the nature of certain advances being made to him. The man edged closer and closer to Benny on the sofa. First there was an arm around his shoulder. Then there was a hand on his knee. And then, encouraged by Ben's lack of protest, the gay seducer leaned forward for a kiss. At this point danger signals seeped through into even Ben's sodden brain, and it dawned on him that the job he was auditioning for depended entirely on his willingness to perform off stage rather than on. Amazed and horrified, he fled.

'I know it seems crazy nowadays, but I honestly did not know about such things. And when he came and sat close to me I thought he was just being matey,' Benny told me, chuckling at his own naivety.

Come to think of it, he was queer. Very queer. But never even the tiniest bit homosexual. Actually I don't think his sex drive was that great at all. But he did sleep with various women in his life, and I knew that for certain. Occasionally he would say something, or a girl would say something, or there would be some little incident which would leave me in no doubt whatsoever what had been going on.

In our early days together I learned that the gently understated phrase: 'She's very friendly to me, Den,' usually indicated a sexual relationship. If he phoned me and said: 'Don't come around. I'm a busy boy,' that also usually indicated that he was entertaining a lady whom he expected to end up in bed with.

In later years, as he grew older and even further set in his ways, I think he more or less stopped seeking out sexual encounters. But that is not an unusual pattern of behaviour. And although another theory about Ben is that he was completely asexual, I can guarantee that was not true in his earlier years.

He loved women in every way, actually, and much preferred their company to that of men. His physical preference was for small, dark women, both on and off screen, yet somehow the world always has an image of him surrounded by buxom blondes. When he went to America to film for the show we did for Don Taffner, we needed four or five girls for a scene in a park. We were taken to this audition room full of gorgeous-looking girls, but they all had the most enormous boobs we had ever seen.

'Your kind of girls, eh Benny?' said the casting director, full of confidence. And we had to explain tactfully that we were looking for normally built, pretty girls whom any man would turn to look at if they walked past.

Away from work, Benny still preferred to be with women who were in showbusiness in some form or another. Then he could chatter on about the business, as he liked to do, and enjoy the presence of a pretty girl at the same time.

He occasionally took girls abroad with him on his travels, but he didn't find that entirely satisfactory. They were inclined to be too demanding of him. Few girls taken to Paris for a weekend would want to spend their evenings sitting in their five star hotel room watching French TV.

But that was Ben. He was one of the world's great lunchers, of course – he loved lavish lunches. But at night he always wanted to watch TV. Then sometimes he would get an idea for a sketch and he would start scribbling, sit up until dawn and then want to sleep all morning. What he wouldn't want then was somebody nagging him to go sightseeing.

And that was one of the reasons why he usually preferred to travel either alone or with me, just a mate whom he worked with. He loved to show off his knowledge of a place to someone, to entertain you in the best restaurant in town, and all of that. But when he had done all he wanted of that, he just wanted to be left alone. And if Ben settled down to overdose on the local TV or burn the midnight oil dreaming up new gags, I would quite happily tootle off and do my own thing for a few hours. I wouldn't bother him. So that made me an acceptable travelling companion.

But Ben knew women all over the world. His ideal was to turn up in Rome or New York or wherever, take some lovely girl out to a lovely lunch, and then, when he wanted, take her home and be shot of her. He did not want to be stuck with someone who might try to impose their will on him.

When he was very young he once proposed marriage to a girl by telephone. It was 1950, and Ben was a twenty-five-year-old comic enjoying his first real break in showbusiness. He was playing straight man to Reg Varney in a revue called *Gaytime* at the Lido, Clifton-ville, on the outskirts of Margate. He began to date a young soubrette – the name for the female performers of those days who could sing, dance and act and were stalwarts of revenues – from another Margate show, and fell for her heavily.

Ben was determined to make her his wife. But he did not have the courage to ask her face to face. He decided the deed must be done on the telephone, and the phone at his digs would not do, because the landlady would overhear.

'So I went to a public callbox on Margate Front,' recalled Benny. 'I chatted up my girlfriend for a bit, and then popped the question, "Will you marry me?"

'I knew from her reaction I'd done the wrong thing. She was very sweet about it and even pretended she cared by asking me to give her twenty-four hours to think it over. The next day we spoke again on the phone, and this time she told me that, much as she liked me, she didn't love me enough to marry me. So that was that. She married someone else and left the business. I often look back and wonder how different my life might have been had she accepted me. I wasn't making much headway in showbusiness then. She might have persuaded me to leave it. I could have finished up a banker.'

I would not have thought that was very likely, but Benny was always hard hit by rejection. And he did admit to me that he behaved badly that summer at Cliftonville. He was moody and uncommunicative with the other performers, including his partner Reg, and – typically Ben – he told nobody what was wrong.

Years later the soubrette contacted Ben and asked him to visit her and meet her husband, a Harley Street dental surgeon, and her children. This time it was Ben who said no thank you. Very politely he turned down the invitation.

Bill Randall, a variety stalwart who was once Ben's pianist, remembers Ben expressing great love for Cherry Lind, a famous actress and singer of the 1950s. 'That's a girl I'd like to marry,' he said.

In his forties Ben again fell in love. He was twice engaged to be married – each time to a dancer from his BBC TV show.

Many years afterwards he remembered: 'I was engaged to each of them. One romance lasted three years, and the other five. They were lovely ladies and I was very much in love.

'I'm sure they were both very fond of me, but for them it was never the real thing. There was nothing coming back to me. I was the romantic one, and the love was all on my side. I was close to them, but they were never close to me. You can't force anyone to love. If it doesn't happen, there's nothing you can do.

'After I'd been jilted for the second time there came the great sad period of my life – I was very depressed. I still had to go on TV and make jokes. I didn't tell anyone, but it took me three years to get over it.

'Both of my former fiancées are now married. They're both on TV quite often. They gave up dancing and turned to straight acting.'

Three rejections were bound to leave him devastated. He was terribly hurt.

One of the girls was Australian-born dancer turned actress Annette André, now fifty years old and the star of the hit TV show *Randall and Hopkirk Deceased*. She has retained a greaat affection for Benny, and talked to him only a few days before he died. She telephoned him from her Californian home after hearing that he was being treated in the Brompton Hospital in London for a heart attack.

'I phoned him because I was upset he was ill,' she says. 'I hadn'tt been in touch with him for many years except for passing my regards on through other colleagues.

'He sounded verry up and said he was feeling much better and that was all. I think he was a bit surprised to hear from me. It was voices from the past.'

Annette treasured her time with Ben and says: 'He was awfully nice, he seemed very fond of me.

'We had a good time. We had a lot of laughs together, but he was quietly funny and he didn't feel he had to be funny all the time – certainly not with me.'

Benny and Annette met in what was for him the usual way. She worked on several of his TV shows in the mid-sixties. They began to date, and Benny took her out to dinner in his favourite London restaurants. Benny asked her to marry him over a candle-lit meal. Knowing the romantic fool, I'm certain he would have arrived with flowers and chocolates, the lot – as long as he hadn't eaten half of them on the way.

Annette recalls the night he proposed to her and what happened afterwards in much the same way that Benny did – but she had no idea that he felt he was jilted.

'He suggested marriage. I can't remember what he said now. It was mentioned, and then very gently not gone through with.

'Basically I was too young at the time and my own career was just starting. It just wasn't right. Not the right combination.

'There was never any big showdown or anything. He was fine about it. There was no problem. To me he was a friend, and that was it.'

But I know that Benny took her rejection and the others far more to heart than Annette realized. She eventually married American producer Arthur Weingarten in 1989, and has a twelve-year-old daughter from a previous long-term relationship. I don't think Benny ever seriously considered marriage again.

He used to make awful jokes about it like: 'Why buy a book when you can join the library?' But he could not hide his disappointment, and even in later years that was apparent to me. If any of those girls had said yes, then I think Benny would have got married and his whole life story could have been completely different. Whether he would have been capable of making a marriage work is another question. To be honest, I doubt it. There was never a lot of give and take about Ben.

When he courted he did so in style, even as a young, impoverished soldier. In everything that he did Ben believed in a certain standard of behaviour. He told me a story about him and a pretty French girl during World War II that we were always going to put into a sketch and never got around to.

He was in the army, stationed in France, and he had his eye on this young lady who worked behind the NAAFI counter. In fact he was quite besotted by her. Every now and again a travelling cinema used to arrive to entertain the troops, and Benny plucked up the courage to ask the girl, whose name was Maria, if she would like to go to the cinema with him. She agreed, and Benny was delighted.

Then he set about organizing it properly, as Benny always would. First he bought two tickets in advance so that everything would go smoothly and he wouldn't have to queue up or, horror of horrors, maybe not be able to get seats at all. He sought out just the right café to take her for a drink first, he saved up his dough to buy her a box of chocolates, and then he poshed himself up so that he looked immaculate for the big night out. He had arranged to meet her at the NAAFI when she came off duty, so in he walked clutching his chocs. 'Hello,' he said, trying to look confident. 'I wondered if you'd care to have a drink or a cup of coffee or something in the café across the street before we go to the cinema?'

Marie looked very embarrassed, and Benny was aware of another soldier also waiting by the NAAFI counter.

'Well, actually,' she said, 'I've also promised this guy that I will go to the movies with him.'

Now that sort of behaviour totally offended Benny. He would never have done anything like that. An invitation was an invitation, and she had apparently accepted one from both of them. So he looked at this other soldier, and he appeared pretty fed up too. There was no aggravation between the two men. They just felt let down by the girl.

So Ben said to the second soldier: 'Have you got tickets?'

'No, I haven't,' he replied despondently.

'I have,' said Benny. 'Would you like to be my guest?'

'Yes, I would,' said the soldier. And off they walked together, leaving the girl stranded – which Benny felt served her right for trying on the three-card trick.

He was always courteous and considerate with women, and expected to be treated the same way. But whereas he was a perfect exponent of the old-fashioned art of courtship it was probably just as well that he never got much further than a series of romantic nights out. He would not have suited family life, I am sure. And I believe Benny was really well aware of that, certainly in his later years. He would have been near impossible to live with on a long-term basis. He didn't like people around him all the time, crowding him.

He loved children but he was useless with them – he just spoiled them endlessly. His idea of dealing with a naughty child was to give it another bag of sweets, and then another, and so on. He used to like coming to my house and being with my family, and visiting Hill's Angels dancer Sue Upton and her husband and children. Benny treated her family as a kind of substitute family of his own – as he did mine. And he used occasionally to express envy of other people's family life. But I don't think he really meant it – I don't think he truly envied us.

On a whim, occasionally, he might have thought how nice it must be to have the warmth and companionship of a wife, and what fun it would be to have kiddies to play with at the end of the day. But that was when he was at my house or Sue's, secure in the knowledge that, when the little darlings got over-excited and started biting his ankles, Mummy would be right there to take them away.

And so the way Benny lived suited him perfectly. He was born to be a bachelor. And that is exactly what he was, an old-fashioned bachelor who believed there was only one way of doing anything – his way.

I don't know how happy he was, because I don't know if great comics are ever capable of true happiness. Thames Light Entertainment boss Phillip Jones, always such a supporter of Benny's, puts it this way: 'I am quite sure Benny was about as happy as any comedian can be. He was, at least, content. He lived life the way he wanted it. And he gained the success he strove for in his work – which was the most important thing of all for him.'

Sue Upton says of Benny: 'He sometimes imagined that he wanted a home and family – but really he didn't want anyone to come that close.'

Of all the Hill's Angels dancers Sue was without doubt the one Benny was closest to. They were great friends. For one week every year Benny went to stay with Sue, her builder husband Roger Whatling, and their two young children, Richard and Louise, at their home in Hornchurch, Essex.

'We became the family he never had,' says Sue, now in her mid-thirties. 'He used to call me "mummy". He would say, "Come on, mummy, let's take the littlies out for the day."'

There were various women in Benny's life, for all kinds of different reasons. There was the now famous Phoebe King, who lives inFelixstowe, Suffolk, and Jeanette Warner in Leicester who died in February 1992. Now I knew that he would go and visit these two women – he stayed in a guest room at Phoebe's sheltered accommodation for a week every summer – because Benny always let me know where he was going. He didn't say a lot about them, and Benny did have a way of looking at you sometimes which defied you to ask any questions. It was a look which quite clearly said: 'Now, mind your own business.'

And so I thought they were both girlfriends. It was years and years before he told me that they were severely handicapped and I learned what these visits were really about. That was typical Benny. Anything he did for charity, any good deeds, were always private. Unlike a lot of artists he never wore a T-shirt saying: 'Look at me. I'm dancing.'

Unfortunately, the Phoebe relationship has been rather misconstrued since his death. Without doubt they were very close, and Phoebe faithfully repeated things Benny said to her on many occasions. I can just hear him saying: 'You are my number one girl.' That is exactly what he would say, and did not indicate a romantic relationship. And I believe totally that he promised to leave her money in his will. I believe that he meant to do so, as with several other people, but it was not to be.

He and Phoebe became friends in the early 1950s when she was only fifteen. He replied to a fan letter from her after she saw him perform in Uxbridge in north-west London, and their friendship developed when she met him backstage after a show at the Spa Pavilion in Felixstowe on the Suffolk coast.

Phoebe lived in Walton, near Folkestone, and her sheltered accommodation flat was recently described by the warden there as 'like a shrine' to Benny Hill. When she learned that Benny never did make the will which would have made her a rich woman, Phoebe, now in her fifties, said that she did not care.

'I am satisfied with what I have had from Benny already – a lifetime of friendship and kindness. I don't want his money – I just wish I could have him back,' she said. And I totally believe her.

Benny called Phoebe 'Kitten' and she called him 'Teddy Bear'. Phoebe did not attend his funeral in Southampton because she said she could not bear to see his coffin. She sent a floral tribute in the shape of a cat made of white chrysanthemums, accompanied by a card which read: 'To Teddy Bear. I love you very much, Kitten.' The daft names are somehow typical of Benny. He was a big softie about women.

His attraction to the opposite sex began at a very early age. From the beginning he was a hopeless romantic. He first fell in love when he was twelve years old and he never forgot the experience. It was nearly half a century later that he told me all about it.

Benny always loved the fun of the fair and he was visiting a fairground at Eastleigh, near Southampton, when he spotted a girl in the crowds. She was a little older than Benny, strikingly dark and slim – just the way he continued to like his women best. He discovered that she used to take her father's dinner to him every day at his shop in Market Street, and Benny used to walk the six miles from his home just to take another look at her.

He told nobody what he was doing and would make some excuse to his parents for his absences. He stood in Market Street until she arrived, gazed at her adoringly, waited for her to deliver the meal to her father, and then watched her leave. Benny did this for several months and never once plucked up the courage to talk to the girl. Who knows? Maybe his romantic dream would have been shattered if he had.

In fact, that is more or less what did happen four years later, when Benny was sixteen. He saw his first love outside a cinema, and, bigger and bolder by then, invited her to the pictures with him. They sat side by side holding hands in the dark, and the result for Benny was sorry disappointment.

'I don't know what I expected of the poor girl, but I didn't feel a thing,' he told me, chuckling at the memory. 'There was no magic. Not the tiniest bit of fire. I remember sitting there thinking that I had walked all of those miles and miles, wasted days of my life, for absolutely nothing. Funny, really.'

It could be that Benny never stopped expecting too much from the women he fell for. He placed them on pedestals. And how could you ever share family life with a plaster dream?

The emotional ups and downs of marriage would have frightened Benny. The reality would have bewildered him. He did right to keep his women at a distance. And they did right to turn him away. Ben knew that too, in the end. Annette André and the other dancer he was engaged too were once on television at the same time, on different channels. Ben told me how he tested his reactions to them by watching them both, switching from channel to channel.

And he said: 'The happy memories came flooding back – but, to my surprise really, there were no regrets.'

SEVEN

BIRTH OF A COMIC

Benny Hill was born Alfred Hawthorne Hill in a flat above a lamp shop in Bernard Street, Southampton, on 21 January 1924. He changed his name when he started to act and play music hall professionally.

Alfred Hill was too formal a name, better suited to a small town accountant. His family all called him Alfie, so he started off as Alfie Hill – but he reckoned it looked second-rate on a theatre bill. Try as he might, he just could not imagine 'Alfie Hill' in lights above the London Palladium. The name was just not right for a star – and this young man was quite determined that was what he was going to be. 'Sounds like a cheap barrow boy,' he muttered. The third obvious alternative was Alf Hill. But that sounded like a bus stop. Hawthorne Hill or Alf Hawthorne were not even serious considerations.

So our would-be variety superstar decided on radical action. He borrowed 'Benny' from the great American comic Jack Benny, simply because he was a fan. 'And when I put it together, "Benny Hill" had a good ring to it, just right,' Ben would recall. The sound of a name, the right ring to a turn of phrase, was always important to Benny Hill.

All his life Benny had a fascination with curious sounds which could make him chuckle with glee. He never let up. If he squashed a plastic bottle you would see him listening to the crunching sound. If it appealed to him he would repeat the operation again and again until it sparked the idea for a sketch. And he would go on and on repeating and practising until he got that sound absolutely spot on for whatever magical piece of nonsense his eternally fertile imagination was conjuring up.

Benny's father, also Alfred, and his grandfather, Henry, had been circus clowns in their youth. And maybe some of Ben's enormous talent came from them. From all accounts he was a much kinder and more gentle man than his father. Alfred senior was not an easy sort of chap. But then his was not an easy life.

His childhood was constantly disrupted as his ever-struggling family moved from town to town, usually in the middle of the night, dodging the legions of creditors on their tail. In later years fortunes changed for Grandfather Hill, and as he grew older he became an affluent pillar of society. This improvement in his status was due to his establishment as a respected dentist – which was a little disconcerting as he had absolutely no formal medical training. Apparently in those days anybody could set themselves up as a dentist. And Grandfather Hill did so with marked success.

Alfred Senior was little more than a child when he followed the first family trade and started to work in the circus, undertaking all kinds of jobs before graduating to be a clown. He retained the ability to perform many of his circus tricks, and years later would amuse his children by making himself up as a clown and walking upstairs on his hands.

Yet there was a darker side to Alfred Hill. He felt life hadn't treated him quite right and had something of a chip on his shoulder. As a young man he joined the army, serving during World War I in France, where he was gassed, and in Belgium where he was taken prisoner and half starved in a prison camp. He survived. And when he returned home to Southampton in 1919 he could be forgiven for hoping that the world might go his way for a bit. It didn't really.

Benny remembered his father again and again telling the story of how he was offered a partnership in a shop selling surgical and rubber goods. Benny's grandfather, by then comfortably off, would not give him the small loan he needed, and Alfred became an employee instead of a partner. Eventually he was made manager, leading to the inevitable schoolboy jibe: 'Hilly's dad sells French letters.'

But the business proved to be no joke. It prospered, and the man who had offered Alfred the partnership became a millionaire. Benny's father always resented that. His resentment probably showed itself in the way he treated his children.

Alfred Hill loved his three children in his way – Benny had an elder brother and a younger sister – but it was an awkward way. He would rarely praise them or show pride in them. I always got the impression that Benny did not really like his father very much, and certainly there was not much warmth there. Then again, I know that when his father died Ben felt guilty that he perhaps hadn't made as much effort as he could have done.

Benny called his ex-military father 'The Captain', as did the entire family, and it seemed to me that it was a rather distant, authoritarian set-up. Benny always desperately needed his father's approval and admiration. I know that he felt he rarely got it.

He once told me the story of how he bought a trumpet with his first wages and struggled to learn how to play it. But his father was totally dismissive. 'Wasted your money on something else you'll never get to play properly,' he said. 'You don't know anything about trumpets.'

Then apparently he just walked out of the room, turned around and said to his son, 'You know what the secret of a great trumpet player is, don't you?'

'No,' said Benny.

'You don't?' uttered in mock horror. Then: 'It's all in the lips.'

And so Alfred Hill pursed his lips, wagged his finger at his son and walked off.

That tickled Benny. In fact Ben became an accomplished musician and went on to learn to play the trumpet very well indeed. He was quite good enough to play in top orchestras, and once played with Ted Heath's orchestra at a very big concert.

But, according to Benny, however well he learned to play that trumpet it would never have been well enough for The Captain. 'If I had become a pro soccer player and scored a hat-trick in a World Cup final my dad would have said I should have scored four,' said Benny.

His father was totally dominant, a very old-fashioned stern father figure in charge of everything his family did. Benny often told me how his father always insisted that he could do everything better than anyone else. Even with things that really did not matter, such as when Benny was trying to help his mother in the kitchen, wrap a parcel or open a tin, his father would barge in and say, 'Oh, give us it here, for heaven's sake. You never know what you're doing.' He always had to have the last word, did Ben's dad.

When he told me these stories Benny used to laugh, but I think it hurt him. And I think it fashioned the way he came to live his life. He was not really reclusive, as has been reported. He loved people, good company, going out, having fun. But he was an emotional loner. He rarely became very close to people, and I reckon that could be because of his strained early relationship with his family.

He adored his mother. But she was totally under his father's thumb and I think Benny was very aware of that. Maybe he even resented the fact that she would never stand up to the Captain or even appear to think for herself.

He certainly believed that none of his family were really that proud of him. It wasn't that he was big-headed about his achievements, although he had every right to be. But to him it was natural to take pleasure in the good things that happen to people you are fond of, and he once said to me: 'You know, I was really pleased that my brother got to be such a good schoolteacher, yet none of the family seemed to be pleased at all when I was given my own TV show.'

When I met Ben's elder brother Leonard he did in fact seem to be quite proud of his sibling. But this was not so long ago, because for many years there was a rift between the brothers and they did not even talk to each other. Benny's sister Diana, who died of leukaemia, in 1984, went to live in Australia and he hardly ever saw her. I don't think he particularly liked her – although, ironically the physical resemblance between the two was so strong it was quite startling. Once I asked Benny about his sister and he replied: 'She looks just like me in drag.' It wasn't until I saw a photograph of Diana that I realized how accurate a description that was.

So, one way and another, they were never a very matey family, the Hills. Without doubt Ben's mother was the greatest influence, and for all the ups and downs, remained probably the most important woman in his life.

As mentioned earlier, it was his mother's dying wish that he should keep the family home in Southampton after her death and never sell it. For some reason his ownership of a modest semi caused almost an outrage. The press seemed to think Benny should be living in a mansion. But it wasn't his style, and in any case he would always have honoured his mother's wish.

It probably annoyed him greatly, but even Benny's father realized early on that his son was a natural comic. However, Benny told me that he would rarely laugh out loud in front of his son. If Benny could get his dad to smile, that was quite an achievement.

'I remember once that he left the room when I was playing about, and then I became aware that he was outside the door roaring with laughter,' said Benny. 'He just didn't want me to see it. He was always like that.' But to the rest of the family – his mother, Leonard and Diana – Benny was well established as the family clown by the time he was nine or ten.

Like most professional entertainers of his generation, Benny's fascination with the magic of showbusiness was sparked by radio and films – particularly those famous Saturday matinees with special prices for children. And Benny was a natural mimic. The talent for impersonation, for actually becoming someone else, and for turning that impersonation into very fine comedy was something he was born with. He also worked at it from an early age.

Charlie Chaplin was his idol from the beginning. Incredibly, he learned to walk like Charlie when he was only three. He was captivated by films and film stars. He learned to pull faces and even as a young child he was brilliant at copying speech. Accents came easily to Ben. He imitated Maurice Chevalier and perfected a wonderfully sexy French accent – very precocious in a boy of seven or eight. For James Cagney he learned gangster speak, and he stretched his mouth to imitate Edward G. Robinson, straining every ounce of power from his tiny lungs to produce that distinctive voice.

Ben would go to the cinema and then rush home to try to re-create the performances he had seen. He could not wait to sneak into his parents' bedroom and practise in front of the big old mirror built into their wardrobe door. Claude Rains' smile called for special treatment. Ben told me how he used to peel an orange and then with a sharp kitchen knife fashion a set of roughly corresponding teeth from the orange peel. These were precariously balanced outside his own teeth, with the white side to the front, of course. A thin moustache courtesy of his mother's eyebrow pencil completed the picture.

Mae West was another favourite and probably the first woman Ben ever impersonated – although there were many, many more to come. The clothes came from his mother's wardrobe, the make-up from her dressing table. Eventually Benny's father gave in and bought him a professional actors' make-up box. Benny loved dressing up. It was the start of his lifelong preference for pretending to be someone else rather than having to perform as himself. He always liked inventing new characters to hide behind.

From the radio Benny learned to sing like Louis Armstrong and Harry Roy. He mercilessly copied comics like Claude Dampier and

Horace Kenney. And, of course, he copied the sounds. He learned to reproduce the sounds of almost anything from dogs barking to birds singing. The rumble of a heavy truck, the roar of a fast car, squealing tyres, screaming brakes, a cat purring with pleasure or hissing in anger – all these were music to Benny, and music he determinedly learned to play. Benny's party piece was a sound-only walk involving a golf ball hitting various animals and all the resulting noisy chaos. I once got Benny to demonstrate this for me. He had not forgotten it.

Strange, then, that with all this talent overspilling at home Benny was, as a young boy, totally unable to perform in public. At Richard Taunton School in Southampton he appeared only once on stage, as a rabbit in *Alice in Wonderland*. He was suitably dressed up and had to wiggle his ears and loudly pronounce "Ere, 'Ere,' in the famous trial sequence. It would seem tailor-made for Benny – fancy dress and a bad pun. But Ben hated it.

His genuine shyness was one of his paradoxes. Great entertainer that he was, he remained terrified of live audiences to the end. And that was one of the reasons why television suited him as much as he suited it. The camera, strangely enough, removed much of the fear.

And so young Ben stood miserably in the arc light, head down, cheeks flushed, and ineffectively mumbled his two words. It was a disaster and Ben, destined to become a world-famous performer, never got a second chance of stardom at school.

His performances on the football field were more memorable, apparently. Ben played in goal. And although his ability to stop the ball going into the net was highly questionable, his talent for acting the part was breathtaking. He prowled about the goal mouth like a young gorilla, arms hanging before him, half crouched, as menacingly as he could manage – which was not very menacing at all. It was entertaining, and Ben was unwittingly the star of the show. When he dived for the ball he did so with spectacular upheaval, boots flailing dangerously in the air. And many modern footballers might be more convincing when they take a dive if they could copy the performance of the young Benny Hill. A bang on the leg, and, of course, every goal scored by the opposition, called for an Oscar-winning display.

Ben never forgot his first proper public performance before an audience of strangers – if you don't count those stumbled two words in the school play. It was in a Southampton air raid shelter, shortly after the outbreak of World War II, the citizens cowering from the German bombs took it in turns to stage impromptu cabaret for each other in order to take their minds off what was going on above their heads. Benny had yet to write the wonderfully original material which became his great strength. That night his jokes were as old as the vault under Catchcold Tower on the old town walls, which had been turned into a big shelter.

'I don't like this corned beef – we've had too much of it already,' he said. 'My dad told me not to go on about it. "We put up with it in the last war," he said. But I had to tell him: "Well, it wasn't so bad then. At least it was fresh."'

Benny had at that time just abandoned his unimpressive school career. To his parents' despair, he left without even taking his school certificate. At school, lessons and learning had always taken second place to the radio, to the cinema, to longed-for nights at the music halls and variety theatres, and to his own particular style of wheeler-dealing. Benny wanted independence even in those days – and that meant making money of his own.

And so he developed the usual schoolboy antics of swopping cigarette cards and even cigarettes into a lucrative business. He used the discarded fourteen-carat gold nibs from old fountain pens to start himself dealing in gold coins and then small jewellery. He ended up buying and selling semi-precious stones, goodness knows how.

Full of the confidence of a fifteen-year-old totally unqualified school-leaver, Benny had already decided he wanted to be a full-time entertainer. His father, who loved variety himself and worked as a part-time critic for a trade magazine, had always happily supplied his son with tickets to local theatres and music halls whenever possible. Now he began to regret it. He arranged to take Ben on a backstage tour of the Southampton Hippodrome to show the lad the squalid side of entertaining, the cramped and dirty dressing rooms, and the tired, broken old men no longer even dreaming of the big time.

It didn't work. Benny was just further captivated. He could see no further than the magic of it all – and, come to think of it, he always remained like that. Beginners' luck struck, and he won himself an audition with a local semi-professional troupe known as Bobbie's Concert Party. They were not over-impressed by the young Ben, but they needed someone for a couple of short spots in a series of six imminent shows and he was duly hired.

The main part of his act featured Ben playing a clergyman – an idea he admitted he stole from a touring comic he saw at the Hippodrome. His mother made him a dog collar and a flat parson's hat. And Benny let rip. 'Will all the ladies bringing eggs for the harvest festival please lay them in the vestry,' he cried. 'The young mothers' club seems to have a shortage of young mothers – in spite of all the efforts by myself and the bishop.'

He was too young for most of his material, but he tried hard. None the less, after the six shows were over Ben was out in the cold again.

His family decided he definitely needed a day job, and Benny obediently found his first proper job as a weighbridge clerk with the Phoenix Coal and Coke Company in Southampton. Then his father engineered an opening with Woolworth's, the cheap and popular department store of the moment, which he believed could provide much-needed opportunities for his younger boy. Benny became the resident gofer at the Eastleigh store. He fetched and carried and made the tea, and it was generally good practice for his first theatre job when, as an assistant stage manager, he was also a glorified gofer. He was not particularly happy at Woolworth's, and there was one part of the job he understandably loathed. He had to clear up any mess left behind by dogs brought into the store.

So Benny started looking around for something else and found his most famous non-showbiz job of all. He became a milkman with Hann and Son's Dairy in Eastleigh. He was taken on as an assistant milkman and taught how to look after and then drive the horses, which were then still used to pull the carts that delivered the milk.

The war was underway and men were in short supply. After only a few months Benny was appointed a milkman proper with his own horse, a dear old mare called Daisy who was without doubt an early great love of his life. Benny adored being a milkman. His family were horrified that he had thrown up his golden opportunity to rise to the top of a major store chain to drive a horse and cart around the streets of Eastleigh.

'No future in it. You'll end up the sorry one,' the Captain warned his son darkly.

Ben didn't care. He rode the streets of Eastleigh and let his imagination run riot. One day he was Wyatt Earp cleaning up the town. The next he was Billy the Kid running riot aboard a hijacked stagecoach. And of course it was his milkie days which stayed so implanted in Benny's memory that all those years later he wrote and recorded his most famous and successful song, 'Ernie: The Fastest Milkman in the West.'

Working alongside Benny in those days there was a real life Ernie the Milkman, who remains convinced that he was the inspiration behind that gold disc winner. Ernie Carrington, who delivered milk for the same dairy for forty-two years, now works as an egg packer. 'Thanks to Benny I'll go down in history,' he says contentedly.

They were great times. Benny, still very young, was his own man. By day he roamed the street with Daisy. By night he played guitar with a local band, Ivy Lillywhite and her Friends. Mrs Lillywhite, a music teacher as well as dance leader, saw potential in Benny when he applied for a vacancy with her band. She hired him in spite of his limitations as a guitarist. And he persuaded her to allow him to introduce comedy spots into the band's itinerary. Sometimes these went down well, and sometimes they didn't.

But they were enough to whet his appetite further. He decided that he had to take a chance, that he must go to London and at least try to make a living as a comic. In later life Benny Hill could afford to present a benign and gentle public image. As a young man setting out in showbusiness he was ruthlessly determined and ambitious. He knew he had the talent, and he was not going to waste it. He would kick down doors and sleep on the streets if necessary. A world war, closing theatres and hostile audiences were just around the corner. None of these would stop him. Nothing was going to stand in the way of his rise to stardom.

EIGHT

VARIETY AT WAR

Benny Hill stepped off the Southampton train on to Waterloo Station bursting with hope and excitement. He was in London to start a new life in showbusiness. He was going to be a star.

His few belongings had been carefully packed by his mother into a cheap cardboard suitcase. He had £25 in his Woolworth's wallet – his life savings together with the money gained from the sale of his drum kit, plus a few pounds added by his father. He was wearing the lurid check jacket he had bought for his stage act – it was the only jacket he possessed. In one of its pockets was tucked a folded copy of *The Stage*, the bible of the entertainment industry, which listed all current shows and their casts.

It was September 1941. Benny was seventeen years old. He saw no fear and had no doubts; these had yet to come. He started to walk, and became starkly aware that this was a city at war. There were sandbags everywhere, and piles of rubble instead of buildings throughout the city. The bombing had already done great damage. But for a young man from front-line Southampton targeted as a major port, none of this came as any kind of shock. He was just relieved to find most of the theatres still operating.

He walked for hours around the West End, drinking in the atmosphere. Full of the bravado of youth, he was tempted to head straight for the London Palladium, still the most famous variety theatre in the world, but he had already learned enough about the business to know better.

Eventually he stopped a policeman in the Charing Cross Road and asked him if he could suggest a suburban music hall, preferably where there was another nearby so that he could make one journey and two enquiries. Benny was directed to the Brixton Empress and told that the Streatham Hill Theatre was just across the common. He caught a double decker bus and on the way had another look at *The Stage*. Top of the bill at the Empress was Sid Seymour and his Mad Hatters' Band, which Benny had seen on stage in Southampton.

He found the recognition comforting and convinced himself that he would fit in well with the Mad Hatters, that they were sure to want him. There must be a slot somewhere in a crazy knock-about act like theirs for a lad like Benny. Sid Seymour himself came to the stage door and treated him with great consideration. There was, in fact, nothing for young Benny, but Sid was courteous and gave him a list of names and addresses. And then Benny set off to trudge across the common to the Streatham Hill Theatre, where he was also turned away.

Concrete air raid shelters were being built on the common. They were brand-new, clean and dry. So he saved himself money on digs by kipping down for the night in one of the shelters.

The next day it was back on the bus, this time to the Chelsea Palace. The manager of the touring show there – a man called Harry Flockton Forster – must have been psychic. Nobody could have looked less promising than the young Benny after a night sleeping rough. The dazzling check jacket was not improved by being crumpled. His ever unruly hair was almost totally vertical. His pink cheeks were still flushed with excitement. But Flockton Forster saw some spark there, and he arranged for Ben to meet the impresario staging the Chelsea Palace show, Harry Benet, in his Soho office.

Eager Benny was ecstatic. He began to plot how best to impress Mr Benet, and unwisely came up with his old James Cagney impersonation. Ben unfolded his Cagney prop, a grey pork pie hat with an orange feather at the side, from his cardboard suitcase and set off for Soho. He bounced into Harry Benet's office, sat on a corner of the showman's desk and announced in tough guy fashion: 'You wanna comic? You wanna get 'em rolling in the aisles, boss? You better hire me.'

An amazed Harry Benet was about to throw him straight back out on to the street when he too spotted that spark of something. So instead he sat down and gave Benny a talking to that he remembered for the rest of his life. 'You're not going to walk into anywhere and straight on stage as a principal comic, so stop trying to,' Benet told him. 'You have to learn your trade.'

He also told Benny that the famous comedian George Lacey had started work with him as a property boy on £2 a week. And to Benny's amazement, because by this time he was very shame-faced at his silly behaviour and thought he had blown a good chance, Benet then offered him a job as Assistant Stage Manager and Small Parts. This meant he was a glorified errand boy, another gofer just like in his Woolworth's days. But this time he was a gofer who would occasionally be given a brief walk-on role in the theatre.

Years later, Ben always cracked the same gag about that. 'I'm not an ASM any more. But I've still got the small parts!'

The show was *Follow the Fun* at the East Ham Palace. And the wages were £3 10s a week – twice what Benny had been making as a milkman. Three days later he was walking on air. He had a full-time job in showbiz. On the strength of his first week's wages he quit his air raid shelter and rented a dormitory bed in an East End lodging house, where at least he could have a proper wash even if he could rarely get a decent night's sleep because of all the noise.

As ASM he fetched and carried and cleaned up and made the tea – but this time the tea was a prop used instead of beer. Benny also learned how to mix greasepaint, and he made his full-time professional debut. He came on at the end of the show dressed as John Bull. There was a cushion inside his Union Jack waistcoat to give added bulk – because Ben was slim in those days – and he shook hands with another entertainer dressed as Uncle Sam.

The principal comedian, Hal Bryan, had a sequence with his straight man which revolved around the current national poster campaign encouraging the nation to 'Go to it!' The straight was supposed to deliver as an opening line: 'Hello Hal, going to it?' Then Hal replied: 'No, coming from it!'

Benny had been with the show just a few days when the straight man, who was known to like a drink, did not turn up. Benny was setting the next scene behind the tabs when he heard Hal Bryan start to struggle.

'I'm all by myself and there's nobody about,' yelled Hal plaintively. 'I'm dying for a drink and there's not a soul in sight. Isn't there anybody who will talk to me?'

Benny could hear the desperation. He took a deep breath, swallowed hard and walked on stage.

Knees knocking, he shouted at the top of his voice: 'Hello Hal, going to it?'

'No, coming from it!' came the grateful reply.

Benny never forgot his nervousness, nor the triumph that came afterwards.

'I think my voice was just a high-pitched squeak,' he told me, reliving the occasion one night. 'I was terrified. Hal prompted me, feeding me whispers, and somehow we stumbled through the routine. Most of all I remember the applause of the audience, and then Hal Bryan coming up to me and thrusting a ten bob note into my hand.

' "Here son, well done. You're going to be a trouper," he said. Wow. I was ten feet tall.'

Ben was in his element. He had found the place where he belonged. Whatever happened in the future, he knew he had been right to leave his milkman's job and give showbusiness a try.

The show went on tour and Ben went with it, adding baggage master to his list of duties. After *Follow the Fun* came a pantomime, *Robinson Crusoe* at the Bournemouth Pavilion, and then another revue called *Send Him Victorious*. In between tours Harry Benet kept Benny employed as a firewatchman at his scenic workshop in the Walworth Road in south London. As a bonus he was allowed to sleep there in the room where the hessian was stored, thus saving more valuable cash.

Send Him Victorious was highly successful and toured the country, cheering up its bleak wartime audiences. The show went from the Hackney Empire to the Victoria at Burnley, then to the Salford Hippodrome and after that to The New Theatre, Cardiff. And there, for young Ben, the party was over.

Two policeman accosted him as he waited to go on stage and demanded to know why he had not reported for army service as he had been ordered. Despite his protests that he did not know what they were talking about, Ben was taken to Cardiff police station where he was locked in a cell for four nights.

The experience shook him rigid. 'I was treated like a criminal,' he said. He protested that his army call-up papers had never reached him. He had not been trying to dodge the call-up. How could he be, with his name all over theatre bills? Inquiries proved that he was telling the truth, that his papers had not been forwarded from theatre to theatre.

But by this time the military machine was underway. An armed escort arrived to take him right across England, through London to Lincoln for training. Benny sat squeezed between them on the train, sandwiched between them on the tube ride across London; and, ever nervous of authority and intent on doing the right thing, he was mortified. They did not use handcuffs, but their very manner indicated that he was under military guard. What if he was spotted by any of his new showbusiness friends? He would never live it down.

Benny hated the army from the start, and they didn't go much on him. They didn't come close to understanding him. In spite of intensive intelligence and aptitude tests they failed to spot attributes he had that could have contributed to the wartime military machine – like his gift for languages – and instead gave him a job he was probably more ill equipped for than any other.

Benny was made a driver mechanic attached to the Royal Electrical and Mechanical Engineers – and this a man who could barely change an electric plug. He was a dreadful failure. He was supposed to learn how to service and repair engines. Some hopes. He just about learned to drive, but very badly.

It was all a bit of a shame because Benny wanted to be useful. He was quite patriotic and, typically, he wanted to contribute. He reckoned he had already proved with Harry Benet that he was a hard and intelligent worker. But the army were asking the impossible of him.

He also hated the bull. 'Everywhere I went there was some pillock yelling at me: "You're an 'orrible dozy little man, what are you?" And you had to jump to attention and reply: "I'm an 'orrible dozy little man, sergeant,"' he once told me in disgust. 'What a way to set about motivating people,' he said.

About the only useful thing Benny learned during his time with REME was how to salute. He did a lot of that. And he continued to do so after the war, most famously with Fred Scuttle.

Benny – then Craftsman Alf Hill, No. 14332308 – and his unit were sent to Dunkirk soon after the D-Day invasion. I know that his fellow soldiers soon came to value his gift for languages, because he picked up rudimentary French in a few weeks and became the unofficial unit interpreter. But I never heard him talk much about those days, and although I don't think he was ever in the front line, he was certainly in the combat zone. Benny drove – somehow – right through France and into Germany as the Allied troops advanced and was stationed in Germany after hostilities ceased. The end of the war gave Benny his next big showbiz opportunity.

Because the fighting was over, officers and soldiers of all grades of fitness were now allowed to apply for transfer to the Central Pool of Artists, known as Stars in Battledress. Benny was physically A1 and therefore during the war had not been allowed even to audition as an entertainer.

On leave in England, he went for an audition at the Stars in Battledress Mayfair HQ. He received a warm response and won a lot of laughs from the officers, before whom he performed his latest act, sweated over in army barracks throughout Europe. He was promised that he would hear from them soon.

Three long weeks later, back in Germany, he learned that he was indeed to be posted to the Central Pool of Artists and would be stationed near their London headquarters. Ben was overjoyed as he began rehearsals for his first Stars in Battledress production. He had a part in a musical revue called *Happy Weekend*, which opened at the Opera House in Calais and then toured British military bases. The tour was a successful one. Army audiences at the end of the war were not very demanding and they were just grateful for some entertainment.

After *Happy Weekend* ended Ben was sent to the Army Entertainment Headquarters near Hamburg to rehearse as compère for a variety band show. He had to do solo spots and introduce the band's offerings and the guest stars. But after the dress rehearsal the major in charge of entertainment in the area – watching the show for the first time – called Benny to one side and brought his whole world crashing down around his feet.

'You are not funny, Hill,' he told him. 'Some people are, and some are not. We just can't send you. They'll give you the bird. I shall take over as compère. There is clearly no future for you with us.'

He did not pull his punches, and Benny was shattered. All he could think of was having to return to being a driver mechanic. His dreams were about to be destroyed by one officer. But a sergeant called

Harry Segal, who became a lifelong friend, was Benny's saviour. He thought Benny was hilarious and told him so. He also told him what he thought of the critical major. He did his best to restore Benny's self-confidence and to some measure succeeded.

More importantly, he found a way of keeping Benny with Stars in Battledress. Harry was in charge of an army touring revue called *It's All in Fun*. Three years Benny's senior, he was already an experienced showbusiness man who had been a child star in music hall and was also the show's principal comedian. He took Benny on to his show as stage manager.

'I reckoned Benny's material was almost too good and that he was ahead of his time,' remembers Harry, who now lives in Leeds. 'That was his only problem.

'He was devastated by that blessed major. And I didn't think we should lose him. Anybody who knew anything about comedy could see that he had the potential to be an exceptional performer.

'I said to Benny that he would have to keep a low profile. The major would not let him go back on stage, and I knew that. But I told Benny that if he came with my show as stage manager I would get him performing when we were away from headquarters as soon as I could.'

Harry Segal was as good as his word. Not only did he give Benny another chance, but he coaxed him back when for one decent round of applause the young soldier comic would have chucked the lot in. 'My nerve went completely,' he told me years later. 'That major damn near brought me down. Harry brought me back gently, and it wasn't an easy task.'

Harry first put Benny in the finale of the show, then included him in his own comedy spots, and finally tried to persuade him to do a five-minute spot of his own.

He remembers: 'Benny really didn't want to do it. He was in a right state about it. Time after time I asked him and he kept saying, "Not tonight, Harry, another day. I can't tonight."

'Eventually I said to him: "I've no one else to call on. I need you. Get on that stage – and that's an order." '

Benny obeyed. The audience reaction was terrific, and sitting out there in front was the colonel in charge of service entertainment for the whole of Europe, Richard Stone, who was knocked out by the talented young soldier. He telephoned the major responsible for taking Benny off in the first place and asked why his spot wasn't longer and why he had not seen more of Benny before. When he learned the truth he over-ruled the junior officer's order, and Benny went from strength to strength.

Richard Stone and Harry Segal continued to figure largely in Benny's life in civvy street when all three were demobbed. Stone became a major London agent who ultimately took Benny on to his books and remained his agent until his death.

And Benny never forgot his debt to Harry Segal, who he knew had created a more or less non-existent job for him and then lied through his teeth to get that bogey major to agree to Benny being given it. Many years later, when he was a multi-millionaire and an internationally famous comedian, he paid that debt back many times over, as Harry is always first to testify.

He jumped to Benny's defence in 1988 when the newspapers went through a spate of labelling Ben 'mean' and a 'skinflint'. Harry went to the *Daily Mirror* to tell them about Benny's good deeds to him. And in an interview with Hilary Bonner, which the paper ran over two days, Harry told how Benny had come to his rescue when he was ill, broke and desperately depressed.

'I was getting over a heart attack that nearly killed me, I had no work and very little money, when out of the blue came a cheque for £1,000 from Benny,' recalls Harry. 'There was a note with it which read: ' "Dear Harry, just a wee cheer-up pressie, 'cos yor a luverly feller!"

'Well, it may have been a "wee pressie" to Benny – but to me it was a life saver.

'I was really struggling. Nobody will ever know what that money and that letter meant to me.'

The letter was followed by a short phone call, and the phone call was followed by a visit. 'Ben stayed in the best hotel in Leeds and treated me like a king for four days. He picked up the tab for everything.

'Benny Hill is the most generous character I have ever met, and the best friend in the world. How dare people say he is mean?

'So he walks about with a carrier bag when he goes shopping, does he? Don't we *all* walk about with bloody carrier bags when we go shopping?'

Harry's friendship with Ben lasted until his death, and Harry was at his funeral. It was Harry who was by Ben's side when his mother died, travelling from Leeds to Southampton at once to be with his old mate. And Harry was always inclined to get angry if anybody had a go at Ben. It all stemmed from that army episode. One way and another, Ben and Harry came to owe each other a great deal. The army nearly destroyed Ben. But, with a bit of help from Harry, it also taught Benny to get back out there and at 'em even when the stuffing was knocked out of him.

After the war he reckoned he had earned his spurs as a professional comic, and he had no intention of going back to any other kind of job than entertaining. He paid a duty visit to his parents in Southampton, and then it was back on the train to London to continue his quest to become a star in showbusiness. It was the autumn of 1947. Life had come full circle and Benny had almost returned to where he started when he first took the same train to Waterloo in September 1941. Almost, but not quite.

Then he had been a seventeen-year-old boy. This time he was a twenty-three-year-old man. He had been to war. He had entertained the troops all over Europe. And this time he had £50 in a brand-new wallet and a smart dark grey demob suit, both courtesy of the government. He didn't need a London bobby to guide him. He could afford a proper roof over his head. Just. He had a little black book full of names and addresses – not of would-be girlfriends, but of everybody he had ever met in showbusiness who might be able to help him. He knew every theatre in town and a goodly selection outside. And he had just one aim in life – to get his name up in lights outside the biggest and best of them.

NINE

A PROPER COMEDIAN

No story of a comedian is complete without documenting his early struggle for recognition. Benny Hill had his share of hard times trekking from one theatre to another throughout the country. Life was not easy for a variety artist setting out to make a name for himself. But Benny was a totally single-minded young man. He now considered himself a proper professional comic, and he set about proving just that.

He found a room in a flat in Queensway, just off the Bayswater Road in London, sharing with three girls. Not a state of affairs to raise any eyebrows nowadays, but an unusual arrangement in 1947. In fact the girls were not a bit interested in Benny because they all had steady boyfriends, but they thought it would be useful to have a man about the house. And Benny, for once in his life, was not interested in any women, he had little money and even less time. He was in a hurry. All he wanted to do was break into the showbusiness bigtime, and his every waking moment was spent furthering that ambition.

The city seemed to be full of struggling entertainers, and the music hall and variety theatres which were everywhere when Benny went to war were just beginning to suffer from falling audiences. Television had yet to arrive to deliver the ultimate death blow, but easier communications and a more sophisticated and demanding breed of theatre-goer threatened the survival of the huge network of theatres strung across Britain. Benny's task was not an easy one.

For days on end he used to hang around theatreland with dozens of other young hopefuls waiting outside the tiny, scruffy offices of minor agents, hoping that one of them might give him the nod and offer him a night or two's work. It was a funny old way to do business. He tried his luck at the Windmill Theatre, training ground for so many famous comics. Tony Hancock, Morecambe and Wise, Harry Secombe, Harry Worth and Jimmy Edwards all worked the Windmill. But the Windmill did not want Benny Hill.

He began to play the working men's clubs. An average fee was £1, and for two acts £1 10s. The Soho agents never actually mentioned money – they used to indicate the amount by laying fingers on the lapels of their jackets. Two fingers meant £2 and Benny didn't get that much very often in the early days. Bottom of the pile were places like Tottenham Liberal and Radical Club and Edmonton Working Men's Club. When Ben graduated to football clubs and masonic dinners his rate rose to three guineas (£3 3s) a night.

Sometimes there was a bit extra if you got an encore, but on the whole it was hard, erratic work for scant reward. On one occasion which Benny never forgot there was no reward at all. He walked miles to a date in south London, content at least that his fee would pay his fare home and buy him a cheap supper. When he got there the club manager knew nothing of his booking. There had been a mix-up. Benny never did get to appear on stage. Therefore he didn't get paid.

He had no money. He was hungry. He had to walk all the way home across half of London. It was pouring with rain, naturally, and Benny's second-hand dinner suit – a vital tool of his trade – was drenched. The suit was never the same again. His cheap shoes fell apart, and so did the cardboard suitcase in which he carried the few props he needed for his act.

It was one of those nights when, if Ben had not been so obsessed with showbusiness, he would have packed it all in and gone back to being a milkman. At least you picked up a regular wage at the end of the week. It was, Ben told me, an occasion when the thought of giving up did cross his mind. But I am sure the reality was that he would never have given up, not for anything. And the next morning the sun was shining. He was still hungry but no longer tired. It was another day. A whole new day. Maybe this would be his lucky day . . . .

And so Ben carried on trying. He hustled his way into various theatres and revues – at the more important ones sometimes quite deliberately for no fee at all, because he knew they would give him a good showcase. There might be the chance of a brief radio perfor-mance perhaps, or the opportunity to appear on stage, if only for a second, alongside some of the big names of the time. Then he could invite an agent to see him perform somewhere worthwhile.

After less than a year of this Benny was making some progress, although it didn't really feel like it at the time. He had risen from the working men's clubs, football clubs and masonic dinners to the cabaret circuit and spots in variety theatres. He still needed the club circuit to boost his meagre income, but he did not want to tarnish his newly developing reputation as a variety artist – so he continued to work the clubs but under another name, Bob Job.

Then Benny wangled a week at the prestigious Kilburn Empire and his army saviour, Richard Stone, already established in London as a theatrical agent, came to watch him. The impresario Hedley Claxton was looking for a straight man for his star comic Reg Varney in his 1948 summer revue *Gaytime* at the Lido Theatre, Cliftonville, in Kent. Stone was Reg Varney's agent, and he was helping in the search.

He was even more impressed by Benny than he had been at the end of the war, and he recommended him to Claxton. But the impresario had another man on his short list. He couldn't decide between Benny Hill and a young impressionist called Peter Sellers. He auditioned them both. He still couldn't make up his mind. Eventually he chose Benny – which was probably as good a compliment as my pal had in the whole of the rest of his life. Richard Stone put Benny on his books, and remained his agent until his death.

Success breeds success. While waiting to move to Cliftonville for the summer, Benny was hired to do some radio broadcasts for *Variety Bandbox*. He joined the cast of a series called *Third Division*, written by Frank Muir and Denis Norden. His co-broadcasters were Michael Bentine, Spike Milligan, Harry Secombe and Peter Sellers – who, of course, later became the Goons. It was good company, and Benny began writing some of the sketches. Then *Gaytime* opened and was instantly a smash hit. The Varney–Hill double act worked a treat.

'You couldn't have wished for a better straight man,' said the *Rag Trade* and *On the Buses* star recently. 'We became great, great mates. He was brilliant, just brilliant.'

In the summer of 1949 Benny triumphed again in *Gaytime* this time at Newquay as straight man to the comedian Ron Clark. The next year he returned to Cliftonville to team up again with Reg Varney in another *Gaytime* revue there. They were so successful together that, after their second smash hit summer season at the Kent resort, Benny was invited to be Varney's straight man on a tour of the show *Sky High* which would begin in the autumn of 1950. This revue had already been a hit at the London Palladium staring Jimmy Edwards, and now Reg had been given the national tour.

Benny was always a tough negotiator – totally sure-footed when it came to knowing what was best for him as a performer. Young as he was, he spotted the opportunity to take his career a stage further.

'I'll come as Reg's straight man only if I can have a seven-minute solo spot,' he told producers George and Alfred Black. Benny was so good with Varney, and Varney was so keen on him continuing with him, that the Blacks agreed to the young upstart's demands – but they had grave doubts.

It was on this tour that Ben picked up his own personal share of stories about showbiz landladies. There was one he remembered with particular distaste, who fed her theatrical paying guests – for whom she had little or no respect – second-rate food. But on their way to the only bathroom in the house they had to trudge through the kitchen, where she was frequently to be found tucking into huge and delicious meals which she made only for herself. The lady had no shame, and if any of her hard-done-by PGs came too close she would cover her plate and cry, 'You're not 'aving any, you're not 'aving any!'

The line remained with Benny throughout his life. If you caught him with a big box of his favourite chocolates or tucking into a plate of forbidden chips from the studio canteen, Benny would pretend to hide the goodies and in still accurate mimicry of that landlady cry: 'You're not 'aving any, you're not 'aving any!'

It was also while on tour with *Sky High* – at the Royal Theatre, Chatham – that Ben further endeared himself to his more famous partner. Reg was given the news that his beloved father had died.

'It was a Saturday and I had to go on and perform to two houses that night and try to make an audience laugh,' Reg remembers. 'I was in a shocking state. I didn't know how I was going to get through it. Ben carried me that night and I shall never forget it. He was a very kind and caring man.'

Ben walked Reg on to the stage, walked him through each performance, and walked him off. Half the time he said Reg's lines for him, making it look as if he was repeating something said to him quietly.

And so the Varney–Hill partnership went from strength to strength off and on stage. But the misgivings of George and Alfred Black about Ben's solo act proved justified. The *Sky High* tour played chiefly to houses in the North of England, which at that time had little or no appreciation of Benny's humour. Benny was not even quite sure that they understood his pronunciation of English. The end came at the Sunderland Empire. Benny was axed, the second major hiccup of his short career, and it was yet another blow to the heart.

Reg Varney remembers sitting in the dressing room they shared while Ben was on stage doing his solo. The Benny Hill act had not been going down well and he knew that Ben was particularly worried about going on at Sunderland, which was a notoriously difficult theatre. After a few minutes he heard applause and breathed a deep sigh of relief. Then he realized that Ben was getting the slow handclap.

'It was terrifying,' recalls Reg.

Seconds later Ben walked off and came into the dressing room looking shattered. He was followed by the theatre manager who yelled at him: 'Benny Hill! You're a bloody rotten act!'

Reg was mortified. He thought the theatre manager had behaved appallingly. It was cruel and unnecessary to speak to Benny like that. The young comic was already in a state of shock. This attack was just too much for him and it pushed him over the edge. Ben staggered to the washbasin in the corner of the dressing room and was violently sick. Reg had to watch all this and then get out on stage and win the audience back. The totally unsympathetic theatre manager yelled at him that he now had to make up Benny's time.

Nobody was surprised when a short, sharp message came from the office of George and Alfred Black. The Benny Hill solo spot was to be axed – which was only to be expected. But they wanted Ben to continue as Reg's straight man. To the amazement of all, particularly his agent Richard Stone, Ben refused. He said he was not content just to be anybody's straight man – not even Reg Varney's much as he liked and respected the man. He was determined to make it on his own. Stone, still also Reg Varney's agent, told Ben he should stick it out, that he was getting good money at last, and that Reg would take him up the ladder to stardom with him, maybe even to the London Palladium. But Benny did not want to know. He was never afraid of taking risks.

Reg Varney was as upset as anybody. And he was furious when in 1992 the *Daily Telegraph* suggested that he had been responsible for getting Benny thrown off the show because he didn't want him to have a solo comedy spot.

'Nothing could be further from the truth,' said Reg. 'Anyway I was just the principal comic. I didn't have that kind of control – and if I had, then Benny would have stayed. I would have stuck with his solo act. You could see he was going to be a great comedian.'

It was during his time with Reg that Benny made his TV debut. The two comics appeared together at the Alexandra Palace in 1949, just months after television was launched there. Varney and Hill were in a revue called *Here's Mud in Your Eye*, complete with special effect mud made of thick cocoa. In those days all television was totally live. There was no margin for error.

'It was very exciting, but it was also living dangerously,' remembers Varney. 'Everything was a rush. You had no time for changes, and, of course, you had to know everything backwards, because, if you fluffed it, that was it.

'I remember doing a scene with Benny in that first TV show in which I was sitting on a fence dressed as a hillbilly and then I had to change in seconds to come back as a soldier. It was all one big dash and it was quite daft. On that occasion I had no time to complete the change, so there I was in a uniform jacket with nothing on down below except underpants. There wasn't time to bother about the bottom bit, so the camera just shot me from the waist up.

'And there were no fancy lenses in those days, so if they wanted a close-up of you they had to bring the camera right up to your face. The lens would be about two inches away and it was like trying to look at a pointed finger at the end of your nose. You were forever boss-eyed.'

In the late forties and early fifties performers were afraid of TV. They didn't like the way it gobbled up material. You could take the same act around and around variety theatres for years and make a fair living out of one really good routine. Once you took that routine on television, that was the end of it.

But a greater cause of performers' fear of TV was the attitude of the big theatre producers and promoters of the day. They did not like it. They did not trust it. Entertainers under contract to them were banned from appearing on television, and entertainers not currently working in major theatres who did appear on TV were likely to be blacklisted.

As a result, many of the big name entertainers of the time would have nothing to do with the small screen interloper. The showbusiness world was widely brainwashed into believing that TV would be a seven-day wonder. The clever thing to do was to ignore the precocious fledgeling and stick with the theatre. But Benny Hill was not brainwashed. He saw the future of television from the beginning. And he had an unequalled vision of the scope that it could offer a clever comic.

'Benny developed a special TV technique right from the start, and of course it became his forte,' says Reg.

In 1950 only one in twenty households had a set. And the pictures transmitted to them jumped and flickered uncertainly. But Benny's view of the small screen was not distorted by technical teething trouble. To him the potential was blatantly obvious. While others dithered, Benny determined to jump aboard this thrilling new vehicle as fast as his blossoming talent would propel him.

From the moment he discovered television, Benny knew where he was going. Very early on in his career he told the London TV critic Fred Cooke: 'The future of entertainment lies with television. That's the star to which I've hitched my wagon.' And television discovered Benny almost as fast as he discovered it. As soon as he started to write his own material specially for television and bombard the BBC with it, Benny began to take off.

He arrived back in London after the Sunderland Empire disaster dejected but not broken, down but not out. His belief in himself had been severely shaken once more, but not destroyed. His belief in television became his driving force.

He found the cheapest lodgings he could and sat down to write sketches specially for TV – routines that he thought would suit the small screen and use the very limited techniques already available. He already had shoeboxes full of notes and cuttings and scribbled gags collected from before his army days. In his head was a scramble of comic memories dating back to his time as a milkman. He set about sorting and organizing and rewriting this wealth of material into a new form aimed at the new medium he was so attracted to. It was the conception of a way of life, although at the time Benny was contemplating turning his whole career upside down and concentrating entirely on writing, without performing at all. The scars of Sunderland ran deep.

After a couple of months burning the midnight oil, Benny had forty sketches written out in longhand. He arrived unannounced at the BBC in Lime Grove and asked to see the Head of Light Entertainment, Ronnie Waldman. Intrigued by his cheek, Waldman agreed to give Benny a few minutes. But when forty scripts were unceremoniously dumped on his desk he wondered if he was going to regret his generosity.

'Pick any one you like to read,' invited Benny. He didn't want the BBC boss to think he had put all the best stuff on top.

Waldman, who had seen Ben make a brief TV guest appearance and had remembered him as a promising talent but using the wrong material, did so, but then turned the tables, telling Benny to read it to him. The sketch chosen at random featured a City gent getting into all sorts of bother with the conveyor belt system in a Lyons tea shop. Benny eagerly mimed his way through it, acting out all kinds of slapstick escapades involving the man impaling doughnuts with his umbrella, smashing piles of crockery and falling over other customers.

Waldman casually asked Benny who he thought might be able

to perform his sketches. Benny said he thought the Head of Light Entertainment might have his own ideas.

'Who do you think could do it?' Ben asked.

'I think you could,' replied Waldman.

Benny agreed that might just be possible.

Waldman hired him on the spot. TV was taking off and Benny was in. Waldman called his deputy, Bill Lyon-Shaw, who produced the revue *Hi There!* And it was on this show that Benny became established as a TV comic in a series of solo spots and sketches.

'Mark down Benny Hill among the future TV favourites,' predicted the *News Chronicle* with prophetic accuracy. It was 1951. Benny was twenty-five years old. Television, still in its infancy, was off at a gallop. And so was Benny. The highest moments of his young life had followed swiftly after what must have been the lowest moment at Sunderland. In the manner of TV from the beginning, it quickly turned Benny into a national star. Benny learned early and well the power of television. And he understood it totally. He was already on his way to becoming the greatest comic master of the television medium in history.

TEN

BORN FOR TELEVISION

While other TV entertainers just churned out the same old stuff they would deliver to a live audience, Benny quickly started to explore the ways in which the use of a camera could enhance his routines. He grasped early on that traditional stand-up patter was rarely enough for television, and certainly not enough to carry hour-long shows. In a colourful theatre it was all right somehow to stand centre stage and deliver a string of jokes, but TV demanded more. It called for life and movement. It had to invent its own colour. Television material had to be fresh, imaginative and innovative.

Benny continued to work steadily for the BBC. In 1952 he was appointed compère of a monthly programme called *The Centre Show*, which came out of the famous Nuffield Centre servicemen's club. It was a prestigious appointment. But with it came the first signs of a problem which was to dog Benny all his life. There were always people who found his double-entendre humour offensive, and accusations that he was smutty had reached crisis point when Thames TV axed his show more than thirty years later. Benny maintained that people who were offended by his humour and found it dirty were looking for something dirty and offensive to find.

Back in 1952 he certainly had a point. Producer Kenneth Carter was a little anxious about Benny's ribald reputation in the context of *The Centre Show* with its military and government links, and urged his young star to take care. Benny obediently did his best to toe the line and wrote himself a special selection of carefully vetted material – but it made no difference.

On one show he gave a mock police message. 'A football coupon was lost last night in Chelsea. Will anyone who finds it please contact Scotland Yard, telephone Whitehall home–away; home–away.' It was a joke based on the football pools coupon system operating at the time, which gave one point for a home win and two for an away win. And the famous Scotland Yard phone number was Whitehall 1212.

No gag could have been more innocent. But there swiftly followed an official complaint from Department AG3, the services entertainment unit. Some pillock somewhere decided that Benny had actually said 'Homo-way, homo-way,' and had therefore suggested that homosexuality was rife in Whitehall. A War Office Colonel signed a letter of protest which was sent to the Nuffield Centre Management Committee. The Nuffield Centre in turn took the whole thing totally seriously and demanded that in future the BBC must allow them to check and, if necessary, censor every *Centre Show* script before its screening.

The story leaked out and it hit the headlines. Fleet Street had a field day. Such a piece of pompous brass hat bungling made great copy. A press conference was called and Benny told the gathered reporters: 'I'm flabbergasted. All I know is what the BBC have told me – that some brass hat objected to the joke. They must have misheard me, because they said that home–away had something to do with sex.'

The BBC – only three years old as a TV company – refused to be bullied by bureaucracy. Bewildered, battered but defiant, Ronnie

Waldman decided to scrap *The Centre Show* altogether. He would put out a new show aimed at servicemen and women from the Beeb's own recently acquired Shepherd's Bush Empire Theatre. It was to be called, predictably enough, *The Services Show*, and its regular compère was to be Benny Hill.

It was a popular decision and a popular show. 'Thank goodness the BBC haven't sacked Benny Hill even if that War Office colonel doesn't approve,' applauded the *Daily Mirror*. In fact the home–away incident brought Benny priceless publicity and actually boosted his career. Certainly public awareness of him was now tremendous.

In 1953 he became the star in a BBC programme called *Showcase*, which suited him down to the ground. He was instructed by Ronnie Waldman to concentrate on character comedy and did so gladly, developing the talent for mimicry and impersonation which had captivated the BBC boss in the first place. Benny grew more and more famous. Television grew bigger and bigger.

Later in 1953 Benny was hired by the impresario Lew Grade for a nationwide theatre tour which was a sell-out just at the time that British theatres and music halls, particularly outside London, were beginning to suffer from change. TV was the villain of the piece, providing sophisticated humour in your own front room, and theatres all over the country began to close down. But in Benny's case his TV fame attracted theatre audiences and the tour was extremely profitable. His small-screen fans wanted to see him in the flesh.

One of the venues was the Sunderland Empire, the very name of which gave Benny a severe attack of stage fright. And at first he had agreed to do the tour only if the Sunderland date was scrapped. But Richard Stone persuaded him that this time would be completely different – as it was. He was top of the bill for a start. The show was fully booked. And there were queues of people right around the block waiting to get in to see him.

It was on a long flight to America more than thirty years later that he told me the story of his triumphant return to Sunderland, and he confessed: 'I put on my mac and turned the collar up and put on a hat, and I went out and walked around the theatre just for the sheer pleasure of seeing all these people queueing up to see me at the same theatre where I had been paid off a couple of years before.

'I went on and I did exactly the same act I had done when I was paid off. I couldn't resist it, Den, I just couldn't resist it. And, oh, I did enjoy myself.

'Before I went on the telly they had hated me. A few TV shows under my belt and they loved me. Funny old world, isn't it?'

Benny, as ever, was also expanding his material, always coming up with something new. He was delighted to follow Waldman's instructions and concentrate on character impersonations on *Showcase*. And he looked to the British household names of the moment, most of them also brought to public notice by television, as his targets. There was a tubby TV cook called Philip Harben, whom Benny impersonated with much-applauded accuracy. He also demonstrated his ability to ad lib when the unexpected occurred. A small round potato rolled away from the large roast chicken Benny was using as a prop for one sketch. 'Look! It's laid an egg!' he cried.

The flamboyant celebrity hairdresser Raymond, known as Mr Teasy Weasy, was an early and popular subject for satire. To a sensational response, Benny became Mr Twirly Whirly. Wearing a curly wig and dressed in the satin-collared smoking jacket of the real hairdresser, Benny aped beautifully his larger-than-life flouncing.

Through *Showcase* Benny was earning £300 a week at a time when the national average wage was £10 a week. But he still travelled by tube and lived in a £3-a-week room at a London boarding house. Benny started as he meant to go on.

In 1954 Benny came up with a sketch of a kind which was to become his trademark. He impersonated all four members of the panel of one of the top TV shows of the time, *What's My Line?* in which the panellists had to guess the occupation of a mystery guest. The four regulars on the show – which has recently been revived with Angela Rippon in the chair – were the Canadian actress Barbara Kelly, aristocratic broadcaster Lady Isobel Barnett, TV and radio personality Gilbert Harding, who made a profession out of being grumpy, and the comedy magician David Nixon.

Now in later years Benny developed this kind of routine into a fine art. But when we put together similar sketches on the Thames TV *Benny Hill Show* the show was recorded and we had all the benefits of split screen technology and pre-shot film to hand, plus a budget of almost £500,000 an hour – the biggest in TV light entertainment at the time.

But *Showcase* went out live, and Benny had to change his make-up and costumes in seconds to reappear as each different character while the cameras lingered as long as possible on master of cere-monies, Jeremy Hawk – Benny's first straight man – and the mystery guest. Ben had to transform himself from a younger blonde actress with a mid-Atlantic accent to an older fine-featured aristocratic woman who spoke cut-glass English to a plump moustached man with a grouch in his voice to a balding magician – all before the studio audience. And Benny was magic. The *What's My Line?* sketch fully stretched and displayed his skills – it was a triumph. The *Daily Mirror*'s TV editor Clifford Davis found it 'so entertaining that all the other acts faded into nothingness'.

In September 1954 Benny reaped his reward. The BBC an-nounced that Benny would star in his own show in the New Year. And it would be called *The Benny Hill Show*. What else?

But the first *Benny Hill Show*, the forerunner of such a great world-beater, was not the instant success that was expected. Eight million viewers tuned in, a huge audience for 1955, and many were disappointed. Clifford Davies, who later became one of Benny's greatest supporters, described the show as 'patchy and lacking cohe-sion'. In *The People* Kenneth Bailey wrote: 'The show fell far short of our hopes.'

All Benny's old insecurities came flooding back. But he calmly set about putting right what was wrong. And he began a routine which he continued to undertake every time he made a TV pro-gramme for the rest of his life. He went back over the scripts of his shows, he tried to spot where mistakes had been made, and he vowed never to make them again.

The next *Benny Hill Show* was a tighter, faster, more professional offering. 'Perked up with a bang,' offered Clifford Davis. 'Here was Mr Hill in sparkling form.' Later that year came another triumph when Benny was voted TV Personality of the Year for 1954–5.

It was on the BBC *Benny Hill Show*, directed by John Street, that Benny launched his famous *Juke Box Jury* sketch in which he again used the technique – familiar in the 1990s – of playing every member of the jury. By this time TV technology had advanced, the shows were pre-recorded, and Benny knew from his study of film that there was a way of appearing as every member of the jury on screen all at the same time – revolutionary then. John Street, who freely admits that Benny taught *him* about television, went on an excursion to Pinewood film studios to investigate further. He discovered it was possible to shoot four separate images on the same piece of film simply by blocking off part of the lens for each take. And so history was made.

Benny's increasing TV success made him ever more in demand elsewhere. He starred on radio in an unusual show called *Educating Archie*, which featured a wooden ventriloquist's dummy in the title role. Radio made the ventriloquist's job pretty easy, and Benny played Archie's teacher.

He also starred in the Folies Bergère revue *Paris By Night* at London's Prince of Wales Theatre along with Tommy Cooper. And later in 1955 there was his first *Royal Variety Show* in front of the Queen and Prince Philip at the Victoria Palace.

He began to make films, the first of which was the Ealing comedy *Who Done It?*, in which he starred as a bungling amateur detective who becomes involved in espionage. The film was not a great success and he shot much of it at the same time that he was appearing in *Paris By Night*, further adding to the stress that production was causing him.

Benny was using the same dressing room that his hero comedian Sid Field had occupied a handful of years before. But this did not compensate for the poor reception his act was getting out front. Benny became deeply depressed, and his fear of live performances really began to take hold during his Prince of Wales stint.

But a couple of years later he co-wrote with Dave Freeman – his regular writing partner during his BBC days – a revue called *Fine Fettle*, which was an English version of the French hit *La Plume de Ma Tante*. It was produced in 1959 by Bernard Delfont at the Palace Theatre in London's West End and proved to be another failure. Ben could stand no more. The year after, as a favour to Richard Stone, he appeared for a token three weeks in a summer season produced by Stone in Weymouth. But *Fine Fettle* was his last major stage show.

Movies seemed a safer bet. Throughout the sixties, while he was making his shows for the BBC, Ben appeared in major Hollywood movies in a series of cameo roles. In *Those Magnificent Men in Their Flying Machines* he played a fire chief misdirecting operations from the top of an airfield tower. In *Chitty Chitty Bang Bang*, staring Dick Van Dyke, he played an old German toymaker leading a gang of kids who had taken on a robber baron. In *The Italian Job* he was Professor Peach, an eccentric computer expert hired by the villains – led, of course, by Michael Caine – to bring Turin's traffic to a standstill by feeding the wrong information into the traffic control system.

After the launch of ITV – independent television – on 22 September 1955 Benny began to be hired to make commercials, notably for Schweppes, and to his bewilderment earned more money every year for a few days work making TV ads than he did for all his other undertakings put together. He never felt this was right. He was also a little bewildered, but very flattered when he was asked to play Bottom in a big Rediffusion production of Shakespeare's *A Midsummer Night's Dream* for the ITV network. Benny was amazed to be chosen and more than a little nervous. He proved a sensation in his Shakespearean debut. 'The performance he gave as Bottom was tops,' said the *Daily Mirror*.

Benny was a very good actor, as he demonstrated in his own shows. But he failed to develop the acting side of his career. After joining Thames he made no more feature films. I think he found them too time-consuming. I know he considered trying to write his own film, but he was afraid of spending months putting something together that might not work.

At the BBC he was asked to do a situation comedy series, and he was not happy with that idea either. In the end he compromised by producing a series of sitcoms, but with him playing a different character every week.

It was 1969 when he signed an exclusive deal to join Thames TV. The various ITV companies had been courting him for years but Benny remained loyal to the BBC, making only guest appearances on the alternative channel and steadfastly refusing to let ITV have his already coveted *Benny Hill Show*. He did not enjoy the American-style variety shows he appeared in for ATV. These all had American directors, and at the time Benny felt they did not understand what he was about. He had no control, which he always hated, and so he stuck with the BBC where the early bosses were willing to give him the freedom of expression he always needed.

By 1969, however, the various programme chiefs who had initially supported Ben had moved on and he felt isolated at the BBC. When Thames Light Entertainment boss Phillip Jones offered him a package of four hour-long specials in the recently introduced colour he could not resist. At the time he had ambitions to become his own director, and Thames supported him in that too. He had written a half-hour silent film called *Eddie*, and that was one of the first productions he completed for Thames. Sadly and madly, the unions would not give him a director's ticket – absolutely essential in those days – and Benny felt that only he knew what he wanted to do with the film. None the less, directed by John Robins, *Eddie* worked well and was very funny. But, possibly because his ambitions to direct could not be fulfilled, Benny wrote no more films of that kind. Instead he began to concentrate entirely on *The Benny Hill Show*.

In those days Thames backed Ben to the hilt and immediately set about propelling him to international stardom. They promoted him all the way and gave him an even higher profile than ever. Benny's shows became all-time ratings busters.

His deal with Thames marked the beginning of the most successful time of his life. It also more or less marked the end of all other showbiz activities. Benny had found his utopia in the form of a strictly limited number of big-budget shows – ultimately just three hour-long productions every year. He thought that was perfect. He was always aware of how voraciously TV gobbled up a comic's material and believed strongly in rationing his exposure. It suited his style of working and his conviction that too much exposure on TV eventually kills off entertainers.

It was perhaps strange for a comedian brought up in the last of the great music halls and the seaside variety theatres to come to loathe live performances. Most entertainers of Benny's ilk maintain that live theatre is their power source, where they go to recharge their batteries and feel the adrenalin race through their system. Benny had no such romantic delusions. His experiences at Sunderland, the Prince of Wales and finally the Palace were to him nightmares that he had no intention of repeating.

By the time I met Ben he made no secret of his hatred of live theatre. It made him sweat; it made him literally shake with nerves. He felt he was capable of being much funnier on TV. And he was just not prepared to take the risk of facing another hostile audience – ever.

There were just a handful of guest appearance exceptions on very special occasions. One was the star-studded tribute to Eric Morecambe put together soon after Eric's death. For that one Benny did his schoolteacher routine, in which he has to read from a book. He chose this sketch deliberately because he could have all his words written down in front of him, so at least he couldn't forget his lines.

On another occasion Thames won a big American TV award and were asked to stage a show in New York. Light Entertainment chief Phillip Jones made a personal plea to Benny to take part.

Recalls Phillip: 'I didn't see how we could put on a major Thames show in New York without Benny, so I stressed to him how vital his appearance would be and asked him to make an exception and take part, and to my relief he agreed. Of course, he went down brilliantly. He was a sensation.'

He was indeed. But once more he resorted to his own particular kind of trickery. He did his stand-up spot reading from a diary, and yet again that was deliberate because everything could be written down.

He tore them apart in New York. They loved him. But this was an audience made up entirely of pros in the industry, and that had made Ben even more nervous. I helped produce that show, and I can tell you that Benny was shaking with nerves. Before he was due to go on I went to visit him in his dressing room to give him a bit of a pep talk. It was very humid in the theatre, and he was just sitting there in front of a fan shaking like a badly built prop wall.

'You'll walk it,' I said. On he went, first as Fred Scuttle and then doing his diary bit. That's a great gag, that one, if you are suffering from insecurity. There stood Benny reading from his diary. 'Guess what I did when I got to the airport . . . it's all here . . . .'

'What did I tell you?' I asked him at the end. 'Told you you'd walk it.' He was a different man, of course, when he came off stage. Cool as a cucumber. 'Yeah, I got bored halfway through,' he said. Cheeky beggar.

During the time I knew Benny he turned down the most incredible work offers because of nerves. Live TV was almost as bad for him as the theatre. And, of course, he hated being himself.

He was totally star-struck as a child – weaned in the local cinemas and music halls – and among his greatest heroes were Bob Hope and Bing Crosby. Yet again and again he turned down invitations to appear on their shows. Guest appearances scared him silly.

He would shake his head sadly at his own behaviour. 'Funny old world, our Den,' he said. 'When I was a lad and a young comic I'd have killed to be in the same bloody town as Bob Hope. Now I'm turning the man down. I really don't want to go on his show.'

TV chat shows horrified Ben. In spite of countless invitations we never did get him on *Wogan* or *Aspel*. In his last few years he and I worked on that fear a bit, and we actually did two shows in Spain and one in Holland. He felt it was less crucial for him not to make a pillock of himself over there, somehow. He felt less under pressure.

Ben began to relax a little doing these talk shows, and had he lived I think he might have been seen ultimately on all the big British shows. As it was, the only one he ever did was *The Des O'Connor Show* – and that was because he could be someone else through most of it and also because the show was pre-recorded.

The way in which Ben came to do *The Des O'Connor Show* was fairly typical of our relationship with each other. Ben was watching Des on TV at his home in Teddington, and I was also watching not far away in my home in Hampton. Russ Abbott was on, portraying lots of different characters. I immediately picked up the phone and started to dial Ben's number. I couldn't get through because he was busily dialling my number.

Eventually we connected and I said: 'You can do Des, Ben. You can do it because you can go on as Fred Scuttle.'

'I know,' he said. 'Fix it for me, will you?'

So I did, and Ben went on *The Des O'Connor Show* according to plan as Fred Scuttle, and as the Chinaman and also as an old lady being interviewed by Des, which was cut out because they were over-running. They were all OK because he had a funny hat or a wig or whatever to hide behind. Eventually he came on as himself and he and Des did a number together, but by then he had got over the fear.

He had two reasons for hating live chat shows. First, you can't edit them. If you get into a conversation and it's dull, you can't say, 'Let's cut that out and I'll tell you a better story.' Second, you can't control a live chat show. You can be asked on to talk about your career, sit down, and then they ask you about religion or Vietnam or the Gulf War. Benny didn't want to talk about politics or religion or any of these things. He wanted to go out there and make people laugh. That was what he did. He was a comedian.

He even turned down *The Johnny Carson Show* in America again and again, when most entertainers would actually have begged on their knees and sold their mothers to go on it. But the way things were going I think the next time we went to America Benny would have agreed to go on that show. We would have found a way that he could be comfortable with. But sadly, it was not to be.

In later years he was offered everything by chat show producers desperate to lure him on to their programmes – pre-recording, complete control of editing, the lot. So we did those Spanish and Dutch shows to let him get the feel of it.

The guy who presented the Dutch show was called Evo and was immediately dubbed Evostik, which at least meant neither of us was likely to forget his name. Benny was in a dreadful state as usual. He had insisted that I go on the show with him. Now it was my first-ever chat show, but for some reason I had no nerves at all. Maybe that *was* the reason.

As we were standing in the wings they showed some Benny Hill clips, and just as we were due to come on I said to Benny: 'Tell you what we'll do, we'll bow the wrong way round.'

'Oh, Den, I can't,' wailed Benny.

'Yes you can,' I said, and by then it was too late. I had him by the arm. On to the camera we walked, backs to the audience, and bowed. Then I spotted the audience over my shoulder, nudged Benny, turned him round and we bowed again.

Benny did a Fred Scuttle and got a lot of laughs. Then I did my Tommy Cooper impression, at which I'm rather good actually, and he was very big in Holland then so that went down really well. The audience loved it and roared with laughter, and I rather got to like the applause. So I just carried on with the gags and the impressions, and most of the time Benny just sat there looking at me. In the dressing room afterwards he did a pretend sulk in the corner and he said to me, very quietly: 'Den, can I come on your show again some time?'

The eyes were twinkling. He was thoroughly amused by my moment of glory. But I said: 'Was I milking it?'

'Yes,' he said.

'Did I overdo it?'

'No, you fool!' he replied. 'When you get the chance to milk it before an audience, you milk it for all you can. It happens rarely enough.'

He was, of course, totally at home with his own shows for Thames, but he did suffer with them too. They were his babies. He did three a year, and that was like having three babies a year for him.

At the end of recording a show he never came to the bar for a drink. He left his dressing room with a tape of the evening's inserts in his hand and he would get straight in his car and rush home. He couldn't wait to sit down in front of his TV set, watch the tape and start making notes for me about what should be edited and dubbed and so on. He would sit up all night watching it.

When it came to TV, Benny was the complete professional. And if he had one huge stroke of good fortune along with all that talent, gritty determination and plain hard work which made him a superstar, it was that he was born at the right time. His birth as a comic coincided with the birth of television, and they were just made for each other.

MAKING THE SHOW

Benny used to say that he stole all his own material. 'There are only seven stories in the world, little heart, and Shakespeare stole them first from the Greeks,' was a favourite saying. He was without doubt one of the most original comics in history – yet he would always maintain that new gags and new sketches were almost impossible to come up with.

There was one gag we did once with which he was particularly pleased. Jackie Wright, the little bald guy Ben was always patting on the head, was an Irishman being interviewed for TV. Ben is the interviewer. It's one of those situations where the light is supposed to be on the interviewer and the subject is in darkness so that you can't see him. But, of course we got it the wrong way round.

Jackie Wright says: 'If I was ever recognized I would be a dead man . . . .'

And there he is, bathed in light in front of the camera. So Benny says: 'Perhaps we should change chairs . . . .'

He told me afterwards that he really reckoned that was an

original joke – and we went out to celebrate. We did a fair bit of that.

Benny was actually a master at recycling humour, at putting a new slant on an old idea. He believed all gags were interchangeable and could be adapted for any situation. So Essex jokes are exactly the same as Knightsbridge jokes. 'How do you know that an Essex girl has had an orgasm? She drops her bag of chips,' is the same as: 'How do you know a Knightsbridge girl has had an orgasm? She drops her glass of champagne.'

In reality Benny wrote all his own material for every *Benny Hill Show*. We would sometimes sit down and work out routines together and he used to refer to me as 'a writer's labourer', which wasn't too bad coming from him. It meant that I came up with the occasional idea. In fact we cooked up a lot of sketches together. We bounced ideas off each other.

Observation was the key to Benny's humour. Everything which went on around him was material for his shows. He was never without a pencil and would jot notes on whatever he was able to get hold of at the time – it could be a cigarette packet or a chocolate wrapper or the back of some advertising circular. To make matters worse, his handwriting was atrocious. And I was the poor devil who had to try to make sense of these apparent rantings, often posted to me from obscure parts of the world.

The best one of all was the Chinese one – the start of Mr Chow Mein. Benny sent us a sketch written on one of those pieces of cardboard packing you get in the back of shirts. The writing was even worse than usual and it was just absolutely barmy.

The production assistant, René Bloomstein, and I were completely puzzled. 'He must have been drunk when he wrote this, that's all I can think of,' I said. This piece of old cardboard was covered in words that just didn't make sense. 'Broody gleat trit . . . . Why you no risten?' It was a funny kind of English. Then gradually light dawned. Eureka! Together the two of us cried out: 'He's a Chinaman.' It was just unfortunate that Benny hadn't bothered to mention this.

Ben's idea of heaven was to slump in front of the TV at night with a plate of fish fingers, which he adored. But in the morning the floor would be littered with pieces of paper on which he had jotted down ideas. A ghastly mess – but gold in there somewhere. There was this unruly pile of scrappy notes, some of them screwed up, some under the carpet – and on them would be written these gems of comedy.

His grasp of television was total and we used more visual tricks of the trade than any other TV show ever made. These were the real secrets of his shows. And sometimes these tricks went wrong. Benny was always quick to spot anything that was not perfection.

One time we did a Three Musketeers sketch and we had to film it on an absolutely filthy day. It was actually snowing. But we were on the usual tight filming schedule for location shooting, and there was no question of taking a day off and hoping for some sunshine tomorrow. So we shot in the snow. And this was a reverse print joke – one of Benny's favourite ploys. You put a reverse motor in the camera and whatever you do is eventually seen going backwards, so it looks as if you can do impossible things.

In this case Benny the Musketeer walked backwards to a window and dropped from it a casket of jewels which landed on a plank. When you reverse print a sequence like that it looks brilliant – it looks as if the jewels have flown up in the air, Benny had caught them and just walked off.

Everything seemed to go fine. Then we got this piece of film back and we were in editing. Benny was there as he always was. With this kind of show the editing is every bit as important as the filming. Now, this piece of film looked really good. It had worked. It had definitely worked. But Benny kept niggling away. He made us play it again and again and he kept repeating that there was something wrong. He just couldn't grasp quite what it was.

Suddenly Benny yelled: 'I've got it. The snow is going upwards.' Well, of course, it would be, wouldn't it? After all, the film had been reversed so everything was going backwards.

That sketch did go out with the snow going upwards, actually. We figured that if it took Benny Hill, the perfectionist of all time, that long to spot it, the viewers would be so caught up in the action that they wouldn't spot it at all.

The occasional mistake in that sort of filming is not such a bad thing. Frequently we used to do a number where Benny or one of the other guys in the show would fall off a bridge or get hit by a car. You throw a dummy through the air and when it lands on the ground you have the cameras lock in. Then you quickly take a still photograph – a Polaroid. Then your subject, say Benny, lies down on the ground and you place him in exactly the same position as the dummy. You start the cameras again and Benny gets up and walks away after having been smashed into the ground.

Now if you do that too well it looks quite sickening. Once I did it with little Jackie Wright as the fall guy, and it was so good I actually put some frames back into it so that it looked like a joke – so that the viewers would hopefully think: 'That was funny,' and not 'God, that was sickening.' Benny was a great believer in letting the audience in on the jokes. He would say, 'Let 'em know it's me. Let 'em feel that they are in on the act.'

I suppose the main reason that Benny and I worked together so successfully for so long is that we thought so much the same way. If I reckoned we had gone too far or not far enough in a sketch, I could be pretty sure Ben would feel the same way. 'Den, if you and I were given the same can of film and sent to different rooms we'd come out editing it exactly the same,' Benny used to say. And certainly he did trust me completely.

When we were dubbing and editing, Ben and I used to wreck the place. He never stopped looking for ways to improve every sketch, not until absolutely the last minute. He would watch a clip and then he would say: 'No, Den, it's all shoe leather. I'm doing too much walking without doing anything funny.' If Ben had to open a door and walk to a table and nothing funny had happened on the way, he would call that 'shoe leather'. He would want to be already standing at the table when the sketch began, but if that was not possible because he needed to be seen coming in from the hall to make the gag work, then he would look for added interest. He wanted to catch his sleeve on the door, stand on the cat – anything to get another laugh. Benny was instinctive about this, but I think a lot of big name comedians have learned from him.

Another trick was to use lots of music and lots of sound effects because, if there is a necessary sequence that is still a bit dull even after all the tweaking, you can at least make the viewers feel jolly when they are looking at the picture. The right sound effects and music and even a shot of Benny just walking down a street can make the viewer feel jolly.

A lot of the people who have copied Benny have never got it quite right, because they haven't split the difference properly be-tween the visuals and the music and sound effects. It should be virtually 50–50, because a big sound effect is even better than a funny picture. Benny knew this, of course. He knew instinctively virtually everything about TV.

He would sit in that dubbing suite, drinking out of one of those plastic bottles of Coca Cola, and when it was empty he would twist it and crack it and squash it. Then he'd say: 'Hey, listen to this for the tennis match. *Ponk. Ponk.*' Now a tennis ball doesn't really go ponk like that, but when sounds are distorted and exaggerated they can sometimes be funnier. He was brilliant at sound effects, and he never stopped experimenting. If he opened a packet of tea he would say: 'That's a great crackling sound, isn't it?'

The stuff we were doing regularly was not as easy as it appears to be after the event. Those reverse film stunts called for terrific planning. Benny would walk them through forwards and backwards again and again, talking to himself all the while. Every slight movement had to be right to make them work.

Once, completely by accident, we were whizzing a piece of film back and there was a scene in which Ben peeled an orange. In reverse it looked as if Ben was wrapping this orange up – replacing the peel. Together, as usual, we suddenly realized its incredible comic poten-tial. 'Get me fruit!' cried Ben. 'Get me bags and bags of fruit!' And that led to sketches where Ben would be seen with a pile of peeled fruit – apples, bananas, pears, oranges, the lot – wrapping them all up in their own skins again and piling them into a bowl.

Another Ben classic was the bad continuity film. All the pros love that one. Ben had a series of completely different coats and hats on in the same scenes. A moustache that jumped about all over his face. One minute he had a pint mug in his hand, the next a champagne glass. That sequence, too, was all about bringing the technical side of TV into the humour. And it was uniquely Benny.

We filmed fast, which was all for the best because so much of our material was double or triple speeded that after a really good day's shooting you would think you had twelve minutes or so of great footage in the can – but what you actually had was four or five minutes.

During most of those great years at Thames TV we made three *Benny Hill Shows* a year. The most we ever made was five, and the least two. Benny worked on them all the year round in his particular way. Our annual routine with the shows was that we would start with the location filming for all three, in September. We would spend three weeks doing all the location shooting for the shows – one week for each show. Benny would be picked up at his Teddington home at around 7 am and we would film through until 5.30 or so in the evening, when the light would go. We could have worked even longer days earlier in the year, but location filming in September was a rule with Benny. He would not let anything interfere with his summers, you see.

Benny did enjoy his life, contrary to the impression a lot of people seem to have gained. And in the summer he liked to go for long walks, spend lazy afternoons sitting outside sunny riverside pubs, and travel through Europe. He would hand me a load of scripts, and then in July and August he was off to Madrid or Paris or the South of France or wherever. In early September back would come this bronzed fool who then had to undergo hours of make-up in order to play a white clown.

Every day on location began the same way. Benny wants to see you in his caravan, someone would say, and off I obediently trotted. Benny, of course, had spent the night scribbling notes, altering things, changing a gag slightly to get a better laugh. Invariably he would pass me a huge list of notes and say: 'There you are, little heart. I just thought of that in the night.'

On an average morning he would present us with another ten jokes to throw into what we had already designed. The show was always moving. It was hard work for all of us, but the crews got used to his way of working and we went along with it. It had to be right. That was the only rule.

At the end of the day Ben and I would sometimes sit down with a bottle of wine in his caravan or in a nearby pub and talk about how things were going. But, much as he enjoyed a drink and had quite a taste for it, he never drank alcohol before or during work. Like most good performers, he knew that the little tot which seemed to give him a bit of Dutch courage could actually make him fluff his lines. And he would never risk that.

After the location shoot we would edit, and then begin studio rehearsals for the first show, which was usually scheduled for Christmas. After Christmas we started on studio rehearsals for the second show, followed by the recording before an audience and so on. We had usually finished all three shows by March.

Filming on location was tricky with Ben, because he did not like to shoot in a public place. He couldn't handle it if a crowd gathered around. He couldn't talk. He couldn't think. He could not work if half a town were standing around him applauding and talking and pointing things out. In fact he would panic. He was no kind of show-off. A lot of entertainers switch on, go into overdrive whenever they are confronted with an audience. Benny was not like that. He was frightened of audiences from the very beginning until the very end. And if he did not have to have an audience he did not want one.

What we tried to do every year was to hire a big empty country house that would supply most of our needs. During all our years of doing the show there always seemed to be a lot of them about, often waiting for someone to buy them and turn them into flats. We sought out the kind of house people can't afford to keep up any more – with lots of room inside in case it rains. Outside there would, with any luck, be every set for every situation: sheds, garages, barns, woodlands, lakes, and private roads where you could do what you like with cars without getting arrested.

I always found us a location within thirty miles of London, for two reasons. First, it meant that Benny could go home every night and relax in front of his own TV, which he liked to do when he was filming. And second, I could not afford the hotel bills if we had been beyond the regulation distance out of London. The crew would all have Lobster Thermidor every night for dinner, and Thames just weren't prepared to pick up that kind of tab.

Our locations did not have to be sophisticated – in fact, far from it. When we did the Three Musketeers we wanted to set the scene in France, so we plonked Benny in front of a brick wall with a sign on it saying 'Paris 1 km'. That was enough for us. We were meticulous about not having a telegraph pole or an aeroplane in the background if Benny was in period costume, and making sure that if there was a car to be seen it was of the right vintage. But we did not need more than an indication of where and when a sequence was supposed to be happening.

Just a year before Ben died, while we were in Daytona, Florida to judge a beauty contest organized by Hawaiian Tropic, we took time out to film a video for a CD of his songs which was about to be released in America. And we had a very dodgy day's location shooting at Universal Studios in Orlando. We were trying to film Benny singing a song outside on a sunny day, and of course Universal Studios is open to the public. It is more or less there for the public nowadays, and as soon as we started filming there were thousands of people all around us.

Now Benny was not used to this and it threw him completely. He had a go at me, saying that I had promised him that we would have plenty of minders and that we would keep the punters back. But, of course, it just wasn't possible. And Benny came very close to losing his temper for what would have been only the second time in my experience. He kept stopping and walking behind the camera and saying: 'There's somebody in my eyeline.' Which was not surprising. There were probably two hundred people in his eyeline.

I could see that he was getting very nervous. He was hot and bothered. I couldn't even shut the crowd up properly and the noise was driving him mad. The song was actually pre-recorded and Benny had to mime it, which was something he was very good at, but he couldn't get the lip synch right. There was just too much going on, and he couldn't concentrate at all.

I thought, 'He's going, he's really going, he's about to lose his temper. I must do something.' So I had a word with him and said: 'Look, Ben. We'll cut it short. But there's just this one scene we must shoot here and then we'll move on.'

Somehow he got through it. I called wrap, and said to him: 'Right. We're away.'

Then blow me if he didn't invite the whole crowd to have their photograph taken with him. He stood there in that hot sun signing autographs and chatting to hundreds and hundreds of people. He was determined, you see, that nobody for a single second should think that he was a tetchy artist. He didn't want the crowd to think that he was not a nice person. They had seen him look irritable, they had seen him start to get annoyed, and when it was over he was desperate that they should understand that he had just been trying to do his job and that his problem was that he couldn't concentrate.

I was furious with him. In the end I had to play Mr Nasty to pull him away so that we could get on with some work elsewhere. And even then he did this act of reluctance, of being dragged off against his will. He could ham it up with the best if it suited him, could Ben.

The one time when I saw him really lose his temper was many years earlier at Thames, when I was still floor manager on his show. We were doing a skit on the *Eurovision Song Contest* and Benny was doing all the parts. He was playing the interviewer – who at that time was Katie Boyle – and he was also playing all the contestants.

When he came into the studio things just weren't right, and Benny the perfectionist started to get angry. The scenery did not suit him and needed altering, and the final straw was when he discovered that he had not been given the recording time that he had specifically asked for. Now Benny was a very good scheduler. He was very precise. He knew exactly what you could and what you could not do in so many hours or minutes of work.

He knew that he had been presented with an unworkable schedule, and he just blew his top. He stormed off in search of Phillip Jones, Thames TV's Head of Light Entertainment – a man Ben was very close to and usually got on with extremely well. But on this day Ben was preparing to give Phillip Jones hell. Off he went down the corridor, rehearsing the row out loud on the way. You could hear him ranting and raving. In the studio there was complete silence.

Then suddenly the ranting and raving turned into laughter. And there was Benny with tears of laughter trickling down his cheeks. He had glanced into his dressing room as he powered past it and caught sight of himself in a mirror. He was dressed as one of the contestants, a lady flamenco singer. And there he was, puffed up with righteous indignation, in full Spanish drag: long black lady's wig, bright red lipstick, earrings, high-heeled shoes and a flamenco frock. He came meekly back into the studio and set about quietly putting right all that was wrong.

'How can I have a row with anyone, dressed like this?' he asked me later. 'Just look at me!'

When I was working at ATV as floor manager of their big variety show, there was one week when Benny had to sing a duet at the end with the American singer Paul Anka, who was top of the bill. He had to do it himself and he was terrified. He had to say, 'Goodnight, Paul.' Then Paul said, 'Goodnight, Benny, it's been a great show.' Then they had to sing together 'The Party's Over'.

I remember watching Benny cringe with the horror of it all. Sweat was running out of him as he started to sing. And until the day he died I would use that whenever he was getting a little bit tetchy or nervous. I would sing out of key: 'The party's over – it's time to call it a day.' And Benny would do the same thing to me if I was getting hot and bothered. It was a kind of gag between us which we used to calm each other down.

Working with Ben was fun all right. But it was the most demanding task of my life. I believed that he was a genius, and I always knew that to get the best from Ben you must not try to contain him. You didn't stand on his toes. You gave him as much room as you could. You let him follow his fantasies. You never told him that you couldn't do one of his ideas, that you couldn't afford it, that he was crazy, that it was impossible. Never. Instead you let him dream and improvise and then you worked like stink at coming up with a practical way of bringing the stuff to the screen. That way you ended up with a world-beater.

We did end up with a world-beater. And along the way I needed Ben to sing that little song to me every bit as often as I sang it to him.

FRIENDS AND ANGELS

Benny's team was vitally important to him. The Hill's Angels dancers and singers were always changing. But the rest of the cast of his shows remained the same for ever. He liked to work with the same principal crew whenever possible, too – guys and girls he was comfortable with. And, I am glad to say, he always insisted on working with the same producer and director – me.

Most of his supporting performers had been with him for many years. When little Jackie Wright, probably the most famous of them all apart from the girls, was taken ill and could not work any more, Benny kept editing in old clips of him patting Jackie's bald head and so on, so that Jackie would not feel left out – also, and more importantly, so that Jackie would still get paid.

Jackie worked with Benny for twenty-five years, and became a cult figure all over the world. The tiny, toothless, bald-headed Irishman rarely spoke and was best known for just standing there while Benny thumped him. He was born in Belfast, one of twelve children. His father and four elder brothers all worked in the car body repair business, and at first little Jackie followed them into that trade. He began his showbusiness career as a variety hall trombonist in the thirties, and his curious appearance led to him working at the BBC with comics like Frankie Howerd and Dick Emery.

From the moment Benny teamed up with him he knew he had found a very special ingredient to his kind of humour, and he greatly valued Jackie, who died in hospital in his home town of Belfast in 1989. He was eighty-three, and ill health had forced him to quit *The Benny Hill Show* six years previously – but Benny's kindly trickery meant that the viewers never knew that he had gone.

Jackie and Henry McGee and Bob Todd and Jon Jon Keefe were Benny's long-time partners in comedy. Anna Dawson, a character actress who made her name as Dixon of Dock Green's daughter in the famous old TV series, was a more recent but much-valued member of the team.

The Angels mostly did not stay with him in the same way. Ben was always searching for the perfect group of girls, each of whom could sing, dance and do comedy well. It was difficult, and he was never completely satisfied. Most girls auditioned were talented in one or two of these areas, but very rarely in all three. So we were inclined to use the same Hill's Angels for each set of three shows, and then change them the next year.

Certainly no *Benny Hill Show* was ever complete without his girls. And once we turned them into the Hill's Angels we introduced a whole new concept. There were always girls in Benny's shows, always dancers – originally Dee Dee Wild and Her Troupe doing their stuff like in any other variety show. But in his BBC days and in the early days at Thames the girls were not particularly involved with Benny. He did his jokes and sketches and then they had a dancing spot, and so on. They were not included in Ben's jokes.

Then we heard that in America they were so potty about Benny that sometimes they cut the girls' spot out altogether. We didn't like that, and felt it upset the carefully worked-out balance of the shows. So we developed this way of staging a major routine for the girls which was interrupted by a gag with Benny, and then followed by a bit more of the girls on their own. These sequences, which ended up being nine or ten minutes long, became a unique factor in the shows and proved a big success. It was a clever idea and it worked well.

The girls became more and more an integral part of *The Benny Hill Show*, but I don't think even we realized how much so until the disc jockey David Hamilton, who used to do the continuity announcing for Thames, introduced the show one night and referred to 'lucky Benny with all those gorgeous girls'. It was Benny who pointed that out to me, and we worked on it more from then on. If we were going to develop the girls' act in this way, we needed a special name for them. The first one to be very nearly adopted was the Hornettes. Upon reflection, I think we made the right choice when we decided against that! Then Ben came up with the name of Hill's Angels. In the early days Benny used to audition the girls himself, at his Queens Gate flat in the very beginning and then at the home of our choreographer Libby Roberts, who herself began with us as a dancer.

We weren't just looking for good-looking dancers or singers. Benny wanted girls with bags of personality and he reckoned only he could spot if a girl had that sparkle, that twinkle. Only he would know if she would react to him on camera the way he wanted. He used to audition all the girls individually, which has led to allegations from one or two over the years that Benny behaved improperly. I have already told the story of the former Page Three girl who intriguingly claimed that he had made her his 'sex slave', and once he was publicly accused of 'groping' an auditioning girl. Now groping was not Benny's style at all, and he was very upset. He was, after all, always the perfect gentleman. He might well have taken a number of these young hopefuls out to lunch in a smart restaurant. That would be his style.

Sue Upton – his longest-lasting Angel, undoubtedly his favourite, and ultimately one of his best friends – still vividly remembers being chosen to appear on *The Benny Hill Show*. She was just twenty years old, very new to showbusiness, very nervous and very naïve when she was auditioned by Ben. Becoming a Benny Hill dancer was one of the fastest and best ways into television for someone like Sue. Her agent sent Ben her photograph and she was invited for an audition at his Queens Gate flat.

She recalls: 'We ended up singing and laughing together as he played the guitar. He seemed to take a great liking to me. It wasn't a casting couch. He was very precise and polite, asking you to sit down, offering you a drink, always the gentleman.'

Soon after hiring her in 1976 Benny said: 'Sue is really funny. Finding pretty girls who are talented and funny is not easy. And not all girl dancers are pretty. Some of them look like me in drag. Sue is pretty and she is funny.'

Benny had such confidence in Sue that he used to ask her to seek out possible new recruits for his show. If Sue thought a girl dancer had that little bit extra Benny was always looking for, he would know she would be worth him talking to.

Sue knew her stuff. 'If a girl has flair for singing and dancing, that's a start. But she has got to find the comedy funny herself to take part in Benny's sketches,' she said when she was helping Benny out while we were all still working at Thames.

'Benny is very hard to please, the perfect professional. That is what makes him the superstar he is. I was very nervous when I first met him. But he immediately put me at my ease. He can bring even the shyest person out of their shell. He doesn't especially want big boobs, only if they are suitable to accentuate a certain sketch – like when he leers at them as Fred Scuttle. The girls have to have some intelligence. Too many dancers are just a pretty face and figure, but really thick up top.'

Another all-time favourite Angel of Benny's was Louise English. 'She definitely has that bit extra,' he said of her. 'She is very talented.' And Lorraine Doyle, who also became well known playing Penelope Keith's secretary in the TV series *Executive Stress*, was another favourite. She started working for Benny when she was seventeen years old, and stayed and stayed. By the time she was twenty-eight she was so well established as one of Ben's girls that he married her – but only on screen, in a sketch for one of his shows. 'I can honestly say you couldn't ask to work with a nicer bloke – he's a smasher!' was her verdict on Ben.

The Hill's Angels, of course, spawned the Little Angels, and I can take the credit for their name. It did seem pretty obvious. All the great comics, notably Chaplain, have used kids – and, by golly, kids do get the laughs. But the performer who works with them is a brave man. He has to be very sure of himself and unafraid of giving those laughs away. Benny was always generous. He knew who the viewers switched on to see, and he didn't care who got the biggest laugh. People were not going to say: 'Wasn't the Bob Todd Show good last night?', however many laughs Toddy got. So Benny was quite safe in saying, as he often did: 'Let Toddy have that. He's good at that sort of thing. Give Toddy the big gag.' He could do it because he knew it was his show and, whoever got the laughs, Toddy or Henry or Jackie or the Little Angels, he always got the credit.

The first Little Angel was a toddler called Jade Westbrook, the daughter of former Hill's Angel Jenny Westbrook. Benny thought Jade was entrancing from the moment he first met her when she was just eighteen months old. When she was only two Ben wrote her into one of his shows. It became probably the most famous of them all – the show which won him the coveted comedy award at the famous Montreux TV Festival.

Benny devised a sketch in which he was an artist, and everywhere he tried to paint Jade turned up and got herself into all kinds of mischief. The audience roared. The Jade routine was a big success, and Benny decided he'd like to take it further and so we got together a group of children. Jade was joined by Sue Upton's little boy Richard – the one always in the blue baseball cap, little Adam Jonston, Libby Robert's son, and my daughter Joanna. They were all regular kids from ordinary schools – no stage school kids here – and I think that is what made it work.

It was difficult to shoot, because you can't ask a two-year-old to walk into shot, pick a cup up, turn it round the other way and do it all wrong for Uncle Benny, and so on. There was one sketch we did in which Benny was drinking a beer when the vicar came to visit, so he put the beer behind his back. The Little Angels each got a straw, put them in Ben's beer and drank it. So when Ben brings the glass back it's empty. It's a funny picture – but you try to get little kids to do it. You have to cheat them into it. It was worth it, though, and we did a Little Angels spot in every show for about three years.

At first I wasn't so sure. From the moment we had the idea Benny wanted my daughter, who was about six at the time, to be in the shows and I didn't know if that was a good thing. Neither was I sure that I could cope with five untrained kids.

'You must be joking,' I said to him. 'It's bad enough with one kid, without five of them – none of them pros and one of them my daughter.'

But Benny got his way as usual, and later on I used to tease my daughter and tell her not to call me daddy in front of the girls because I was trying to flirt with them.

The kids loved appearing on the show. It became an annual treat, a holiday for them, and I know Sue's kids – who are still very young – keep asking when they are going away with Uncle Ben again. They really miss it. Not surprising, really. Imagine the joy for a little kid of being in Thorpe Park for the day when Britain's mini-Disneyland is closed and we have the keys to all the rides. They are professionally made up and dressed up in lovely exciting outfits, a childhood dream, and there in the centre of all this is Uncle Benny spoiling them rotten.

At one point I banned the mums from the set because they were trying too hard, but the person I really wanted to ban was Ben. I couldn't always do that, though, if I still wanted a show! But I did actually throw him off his own set occasionally when the Little Angels were around. If I needed some footage of the kids without him

I never wanted him there, because it was impossible with him in attendance. The kids would instantly fly out of control and start yelling, 'Where's Uncle Ben? We want to go and jump on his foot,' or: 'Where's Uncle Ben? We want to pull his hair again,' were familiar cries.

To which the reply was usually: 'Not now. We want you to jump on his foot later on – and you pulled his hair yesterday.'

I remember once doing a sketch in which Benny was the scout-master waiting to take the five Little Angels hiking. He had nothing to carry, and then tiny Louise came into shot lugging an enormous haversack which she carried with no effort at all. But when Benny took it from her he fell over. At the last minute Little Adam decided he didn't want to do it. So suddenly I only had four kids because he wanted to go and play football. Quite right. But unfortunately I had a filming schedule to stick to so I had to cheat him along a bit, shoot what I could of him and cut in and out. Dealing with sensitive comics was a doddle compared with trying to film untrained children.

Benny's feeds were all first-rate professionals. Henry McGee started his showbusiness career as a straight actor and appeared in TV dramas like *Softly Softly*. But his talent as a comic's straight man was first discovered when he partnered Charlie Drake, and he began to build his whole career around being a feed – so much so that he is now universally known as Superstooge.

The secret of Henry's success was that he had no problems with playing second fiddle. And, ironically, playing second fiddle to Ben made him a star in his own right.

Of his days with Benny he says: 'It was very lucrative. I earned much more than I did as a straight actor, and in fact, Ben's shows funded my acting career because for most of the year while I was working with him I was actually acting in theatre. And of course the better known I became through the TV shows the more that helped with my theatre work. I began to get star billing and become better paid. The show was also great fun. My only worry was that one day I would burst out laughing and spoil the whole thing. Because we did do some very funny things.'

Henry worked with Benny for twenty-two years, and is now in his sixties. He's another bachelor, living in Fulham in south-west London.

'Benny was very loyal to his team,' he says. 'In between shows I did not often see him but we talked on the phone. Once you got Ben on the phone you could never get him off. He enjoyed long phone conversations. Twenty-two years is a long time to work with a man, and although I never felt I really got to know Benny well I think I did understand him.

'Nothing ever changed him. He was exactly the same to me from the very beginning when we first met at the BBC until the very end. Nothing ever changed the way he lived, either. I made the mistake once of suggesting to him that he should buy a microwave oven because of all the packaged low-calorie meals he used to buy to eat in front of the TV. "You would be able to heat them up in five minutes instead of waiting for twenty," I told him.

'He looked at me curiously. "What would I do with the other fifteen minutes?" he asked. Well, there was really no answer to that.'

Actress Patricia Hayes, still going strong at over eighty, was a regular member of Benny's team for many years and also praises his loyalty. In 1971 Pat made the TV play *Edna the Inebriate Woman*, for which she won the British Academy TV Actress of the Year award. Until that time she had been regarded almost entirely as a comedy actress, largely in supporting roles, and *Edna* changed her whole career.

In her speech of acceptance when she was presented with her award Patricia thanked Ben for enabling her to make the play. When she was offered the role she was under contract to *The Benny Hill Show*, but Ben saw what a wonderful opportunity *Edna* was for her and at once released her. Pat never forgot that.

Comedy actor Bob Todd was with Ben for twenty years. He was working as a farmer when he started bombarding Benny with letters asking for a job. Benny eventually met Bob and gave him a try. He was impressed. It was the start of a good partnership. But Bob, now nearing seventy, shared Henry McGee's problem with the giggles. During the making of one show he said: 'The worst thing is to catch Benny's eye, because you know he's creasing up inside. And that starts me off.'

Jon Jon Keefe was spotted by Benny when he was doing cabaret in a London nightclub. Says Jon Jon: 'I received a note in my dressing room saying he liked my act and did I want to join his show. I thought it was a joke, but I rang up anyway. I couldn't believe it when Benny was serious.'

Among the blokes, Jon Jon was the newest and youngest recruit in a long-standing team of veterans – which may be why he was the butt of more than his share of on-set pranks. After all, he was only with the show for sixteen years. Once when we were on location Jon Jon phoned up to say he was on tour on a liner somewhere and was going to be a couple of days late joining us. It was my problem. But I knew, although he said nothing, that Benny was not entirely happy with this news. So on the day Jon Jon arrived we decided to have some fun with him and teach him a lesson at the same time.

We all welcomed him warmly and he was despatched to make-up and wardrobe where he was told that he was going to be in drag that day. He was not surprised, because everything changed so fast with Benny. Often one of our lads would be told that he was going to be a Zulu the next day, and then when he arrived on set it would all be different and he would be a Red Indian.

And so Jon Jon unsuspectingly went through make-up and allowed himself to be dressed up in high-heeled shoes, frock, wig, big fur coat and hat, and waited patiently to be called. The morning passed and it turned out to be the hottest day of the year. He was really suffering in all this gear. At lunchtime we decided to go to the pub and I made Jon Jon come with us, still dressed in drag. 'Come on – what's the matter with you?' I said. 'It doesn't matter what you look like.'

Eventually, at the end of the afternoon, I called Jon Jon over.

Benny knew what was going to happen. He was smiling contentedly. Jon Jon staggered across to me, boiling hot, sweat pouring from him. 'What are you doing dressed like that?' I asked. 'The only shot I've got for you is in the shower, and I'm not doing that till tomorrow.'

He couldn't believe his ears. 'What!' he cried. He was so hot and uncomfortable he could barely speak. 'Who do I talk to?' he stammered.

'Me. And don't ever be late on my location again!' I said.

Benny was loving it. He just stood there smiling gently at poor Jon Jon. The eyes were in fine twinkle. Honour had been satisfied.

Later on that same location shoot, which was near Ashstead in Surrey, Jon Jon suffered from Benny's expertise with mimicry. We were on our way back to the studios one night to see the rushes of that day's filming. Jon Jon was alone in his car and I travelled with Ben and our floor manager Fiona Waters, known as Fizz, on the excuse that I needed to discuss the next day's shoot with them. We had concealed a crew walkie-talkie radio beneath the front passenger seat of Jon Jon's car. Fizz had just finished working on the police TV series *The Bill* and was very familiar with police dialogue. So we planned a major wind-up.

We homed in on Jon Jon's radio, and Benny and Fizz started to transmit a pretty fair rendering of police radiospeak. Benny kept changing voices and accents, giving a very realistic impression that there were radio conversations going on between a number of sources.

Then Fizz said something like: 'Victor One to BD, this is Ashstead here. We've found him. We've spotted him. He's approaching Esher roundabout.'

All this was transmitted into Jon Jon's car, and he thought his radio must have picked up the police signals — like they do sometimes. He started fiddling with the knobs, but could not get rid of the police voices.

Then Ben, doing a marvellous tough guy-type voice with a street-wise Cockney accent, cut in: 'This is B42 here. Ashstead. Do not intercept. Repeat, do not intercept. This is a very dangerous criminal. Can you confirm car registration number. Over.'

Fizz, in very convincing style, well trained at *The Bill*'s fictional Sunhill police station, promptly gave the registration number and description of Jon Jon's car. We were only about three vehicles behind him at the time, and we were all convinced that his car swerved violently as this piece of news came mysteriously over the air.

'Do you have him, B42?' asked Fizz.

'We have him, Ashstead,' reported Ben authoritatively. 'Do not approach. Leave him to us. This is a very strange dangerous man who wanders up and down Ashstead High Street in drag . . . .'

At that point Jon Jon's car hurtled off into a lay-by. We could see him searching for the walkie-talkie as we drove swiftly by. Within a few minutes he was on the air. 'Z Victor 2 to you lot. You really had me going. You bastards!' We worked hard on *The Benny Hill Show*, so I suppose we played hard too.

For such a big star, Benny was actually surprisingly sensitive to the needs and problems of the other members of his team – which may be one of the reasons why they almost all displayed such long-term loyalty to him. If he saw one of the cast or crew looking worried or depressed, he was quite likely to walk over and try to cheer them up. He had a stack of suitable one-liners. A favourite was: 'Thirty days hath September, April June and November. All the rest have thirty-one. It just isn't fair!' Gentle, silly stuff. But you can't stop yourself smiling.

Benny preferred to have people around him with smiles on their faces. And he did notice, unlike most stars in his kind of bracket who invariably consider themselves to be the centre of the universe, around which everything and everybody else revolves as best it can. I know everybody in showbiz always gushes about their wonderful colleagues – the luvvie syndrome so neatly sent up by the cartoon TV show *Spitting Image*. But there is no doubt that the Benny Hill team was a fine one. And, by and large, it was a pretty happy one too.

THIRTEEN

THAT SACKING

I still cannot believe Thames TV actually sacked Benny Hill. Not only was he the most famous comic in the world, but he was also their biggest money-spinner. It was extraordinary.

Benny was shattered. I don't know if he ever got over it. His work was his life and television was everything to him. That was all he did. He could not understand – and who could blame him – why Thames should axe the only British comic ever to make it worldwide, ever to conquer America. It didn't make sense then. And it doesn't make sense now. I shall remember how it happened for the rest of my life.

It was in 1989, and we had just come back from a trip to the Cannes TV Festival on behalf of Thames. It had all been a great triumph. Benny was feted wherever he went. His shows were on TV five nights a week in France and he remains a very big star over there. They always treated him like a national hero. And the people of Cannes really entered into the spirit of it. They made a huge fuss of Benny. He was mobbed in the street. Waiters wouldn't serve because they only wanted to look after Benny. He couldn't move for crowds of fans. We couldn't get him into the festival centre, and we couldn't get him out for the hordes of people wanting to get close to him. It was quite an experience.

After we came back to England various people in new jobs at Thames were saying that they wanted to have a chat with Benny because they didn't know him very well. Phillip Jones, who had been Head of Light Entertainment at Thames since the company was formed, had retired and John Howard Davies was the new boss. He contacted us and said he would like to see Benny, and an appointment was made for ten o'clock one morning. Neither Benny nor I had any misgivings about this at all. It seemed perfectly natural that John should want to see him. We didn't give it much thought at all, as I remember. We just assumed that he would want to discuss our progress with the next batch of shows, and just generally get to know Benny.

We arrived at John's office together, and I was asked if I would mind waiting while he had a word with Benny alone.

I said, 'Fine.'

Absolutely no warning bells were ringing. Why should they be? We were so successful, I suppose we just assumed that we would carry on for as long as Benny was able, which looked like being for a good few years yet.

After two minutes – no more – the door opened and I was asked in. Benny was just sitting there. He looked stunned. His face was quite blank. There was certainly no twinkle in his eye that morning. Looking at him was the first time I had any indication that something was seriously wrong. Benny appeared to be in a state of shock.

Having delivered the news so quickly and so sharply to his biggest star, strangely enough, when I came into the room, John Howard Davies started to dither and went off at a slight tangent.

Benny interrupted. 'You can tell him, you know, he's a big grown-up boy.'

Then I was told the same news he had already been given. John Howard Davies put it very simply. 'I don't want to do any more *Bennys*.'

I said: 'All right. Mmmm. OK.'

It was all nonsense really, but it was such a shock that I felt quite numb. Frankly, I do not remember what I said after that. I suppose I must have said something, but I have no memory of what – and the meeting was over so quickly that neither of us was given a chance to collect our thoughts and say anything much. No time was wasted on niceties. Five minute later we were out of the door and walking up the road.

The first thing Benny said to me was: 'I must go home and phone Richard.' His agent obviously had to be told quickly. I think it was apparent to us, even in our state of shock, that this would be a big news story and Benny needed advice on how to handle it. It was also apparent to me that, whatever Ben decided to do next, however he planned to break the news to the nation, it could and should wait for ten minutes.

'You're not phoning anybody yet,' I said.

'But I must go and phone Richard.'

'No, you're not. You're coming with me,' I said.

'Where?' asked Benny.

'We're going to the pub.'

Benny looked at his watch. Incredibly, it was still only twenty past ten. The man's whole world had been turned upside down in just a few minutes.

'Never mind,' I said. 'We're going to go up the pub to have a drink.'

He managed a smile. 'All right, little heart.'

And so we walked from Thames Studio to what was really Ben's local, the King's Head, which we always referred to as Jim's pub after the landlord.

As we were walking Benny suddenly said: 'Hey, weren't we in Cannes last week?'

'Yes,' I replied.

'And wasn't I being mobbed everywhere I went?'

'Yes, Ben, you were.'

'And am I Thames' biggest seller, their number one earner?'

'Yes, Ben, you are.'

'And were we in America six months ago, and was I being mobbed everywhere there and being told what a big star I am?'

'Yes, Ben, you were.'

'I am Thames' biggest seller, aren't I, Dennis?'

'Yes, Ben.'

'And I have just been sacked, haven't I?'

'Yes, Ben, you have.'

'I see. I've never been sacked before, Dennis.'

We bought a couple of beers in Jim's pub and took them into the garden and just sat and looked at each other. I wanted to calm him down. It wouldn't be Ben's way to make a big song and dance about it, but I knew how he was feeling.

'The world is your lobster, Ben, as George Cole would say,' I told him.

Benny didn't even respond, which was totally unlike him. He was deeply hurt. He already had more money than he knew what to do with, and it wasn't that. His whole reason for being had been taken away from him. And after all that he had given Thames, the way in which it was done was particularly hurtful.

None the less, he showed no inclination to hit back and agreed with Thames that the news of his sacking should be played down. He went along with a plan to make it look as if he had decided to quit because he wanted a rest from TV for a year or two. With this man nothing could be further from the truth, of course.

But Benny sanctioned an official press statement from Thames that his show was to end because he wanted 'time to travel around and observe things'. And a Thames spokesman insisted that Benny's demise had nothing whatsoever to do with attacks on his comedy from feminist organizations, and from the Broadcasting Standards Council itself.

This statement was published in the national press on 31 May 1989. And the next day the charade continued with Benny allowing himself to be quoted as saying: 'I'm just having a little rest, that's all. I'm just going to be a bit later than planned with my next show.' But by Sunday, 4 June, the real truth was out. 'Benny Hill did not retire from ITV – he was sacked,' thundered the *Sunday Mirror*.

And sacked he was – in two minutes. If Thames TV management had taken him on their famous boat by the studios and given him a lovely lunch, or taken him to the Savoy and made a fuss of him, it would have been different. They could have told him that they didn't want to do any more shows for a couple of years because they had so many in stock which were taking off like rockets everywhere and selling like mad. They could have said they were not planning any more shows right now, but would think about it in a year's time.

There are a dozen different ways in which that message could have been couched which Benny would have understood. Business is business, and Benny always understood business. But nobody made any effort at all to break the news to him nicely, and I think that was the most hurtful thing of all to Ben. He said very little about it and was rarely heard to complain. But he did remark to me: 'It was a bit hard after twenty-one years to go out like that, Den.'

And his agent Richard Stone spoke angrily of the sacking on the 1992 *Omnibus* programme *Benny Hill: Clown Imperial*. 'Benny was treated like a naughty schoolboy,' he said, with considerable justification. Richard was indeed furious. He felt he should have been contacted first, and that Benny's record with Thames should at least have justified some discussion. For him to have been summarily dismissed after all those years of glory was astonishing.

The real reason why Benny was sacked, at the peak of his powers and of his commercial success, will always be a puzzle. John Howard Davies did not give us a reason. It might seem curious, but we never really asked. There seemed little point. A decision had been made and we had to live with it. The press homed in on the fact that Benny was under fire for being smutty. He was the butt of all kinds of attacks from feminist groups at the time.

However, I never thought that was the true reason. I think it was just a question of a new head of department wanting to do things his way. Wanting to put on new shows and take off what had been left behind by his predecessors. And I think he wanted more money for his own projects. *The Benny Hill Show* was a very expensive show to make. By 1989 it cost almost half a million pounds an hour to produce, which was about four times the cost of most light entertainment shows.

Phillip Jones, his predecessor and a great Benny Hill champion, backs up that view. 'A new broom is inclined to sweep clean,' he says. 'And although Benny's shows brought in such huge revenue, TV is a funny place. The budget that programme bosses are given would not really reflect future sales. To a programme boss you are just looking at one very expensive show, which, if it were scrapped, would allow him to make maybe four programmes for the same cost.'

I have no doubt that if Phillip Jones had still been with Thames Benny would have still been making his shows for them until his death. 'I certainly would have done my best to keep him,' Phillip says modestly. Considering that he was probably the most powerful and successful Light Entertainment boss in the history of ITV, his best would more than likely have been good enough. But Phillip was no longer there. Benny was out. And, inevitably I suppose, so was I. A couple of weeks later I was told to pack my bags. As a producer and director I was not on the staff of Thames TV, but I was pretty damn close. I had worked for them for twenty years on a contractual basis. I then had five months left on my current annual contract, and they bought me out.

At first I was not personally all that worried. They simply told me they did not have a show for me. And I was aware that people were starting to be given show-by-show contracts throughout the TV industry, which was by then seriously tightening its belt. What was occurring was becoming quite evident. Even before they lost their franchise to broadcast in 1991 Thames laid off more than two thousand people, and the signs that those kind of cutbacks were on the card were already all around us.

So I had rather expected that my contract would go. But I also expected that sooner or later they would hire me again on a freelance basis to produce or direct some special for them. I expected to get less work, but I certainly did not expect to get no shows at all. I had quite a track record making light entertainment shows with Thames, and I had won three comedy prizes at the prestigious Montreux TV Festival for them. One for a *Benny Hill Show* and two with Eric Sykes films, *The Plank* and *It's Your Move*. In twenty years I had worked for them continuously. It didn't occur to me that this would not carry on in some, if more limited, form.

But I really was out. Time went by. They did not give me any more shows. And I ended up having to sign on at my local employment exchange. I was on the dole. It was the first time in my life and it was quite a blow – although I was in quite good company. A lot of the top people laid off by Thames lived in my area because it was so handy for the studios, and we all queued for our dole money together.

Being thrown out of work together brought Benny and me even closer, I think. We always had a lot in common and this was something else. The big difference between us, though, was that Benny had £7 million in the bank and I could barely pay the mortgage. But we certainly needed each other. Which leads me to a curious change in behaviour which we both went through. Neither Benny nor I were inclined to phone each other just for a chat. The telephone was business.

Throughout all those years when we were working together at Thames, it would never have occurred to either of us to call the other just to say how are you, or how are you doing. Did you watch the football last night? What did you think of the boxing? That sort of thing. We never did that. We left each other alone. I guess if I had not been the sort of person willing to leave Benny alone – both at work and at home – when that was what he obviously wanted, our friendship would never have developed in the way that it did. But after we were both sacked we used to phone each other every day. It quickly became a habit. Strange, really. I suppose it shows how much we needed each other then. We came to rely on each other a great deal.

During those long months after the show was dropped Benny and I had plenty of time to look back over the years, to think about mistakes we may have made, and to examine in our minds those attacks that we were sexist. Benny never understood that. We thought of the shows as being the same kind of humour as a cheeky seaside postcard. And Benny believed that his shows were probably anti-men, not anti-women.

There was this motley crew of blokes – Bob Todd, who thought he was the handsomest one, little skinny old Jackie Wright, Jon Jon Keefe, Henry, plump Benny himself, all convinced that they were God's gift to women. Even as Fred Scuttle you knew he thought he was the great lady-killer. But in the end the men always lost on *The Benny Hill Show*, and the women always won.

Benny himself never got a girl in fifty years of showbiz. All you ever saw was the chase.

'I don't downgrade women,' said Ben. 'Quite the opposite. They downgrade me. On my shows it's the men who suffer – never the girls. When I was a lad and crazy to get into showbiz I used to dream of being the principal comic in a touring revue. They were extraordinary, wonderful shows with names like *Naughty Girls of 1942*. There were jugglers and acrobats and singers and comics, and most important of all were the girl dancers. My shows are probably the nearest thing there is on TV to those old revues.'

Just a few months before Ben's sacking the government's newly formed telly watchdog, the Broadcasting Standards Council, viciously put the boot in. 'It's not as funny as it was to have half-naked girls chased across the screen by a dirty old man,' announced BSC director Colin Shaw. 'Attitudes have changed. The kind of behaviour that gets a stream of men sent to magistrates' courts each year isn't at all amusing.'

145

Colin Shaw, of course, got the whole thing completely wrong – particularly with reference to the little matter of who chases whom in *The Benny Hill Show*.

'I don't chase the girls, they always chase me. It's the other way around – that's the joke,' Ben explained patiently, again and again.

Earlier in 1987, comedian and writer Ben Elton attacked Benny on the *Saturday Live* TV show. Elton – whom both Benny and I have always thought to be a brilliant writer, by the way – remarked that the number of incidents of rape had increased, and asked how women could walk in safety when Benny Hill had just been on TV chasing half-naked girls through a park.

Benny was very upset by that – not least because Elton's facts were so off-beam that it seemed likely he had never even watched *The Benny Hill Show*. But, most of all, Benny couldn't believe that a fellow artist had attacked him. That was totally against Benny's ethical code. And so he never named Ben Elton or launched a counter-attack against him. But he did say publicly at the time: 'Several of the newer comedians are like little boys at school, blaming someone else for something to divert attention from themselves. Their own material is outrageous, and yet they have the nerve to attack me. I watched one episode of the alternative comedy shows where a naked man was bouncing up and down on another man's lap. Is that a very good idea in the middle of the AIDS crisis? And I was amazed by an episode of *Filthy Rich and Catflap* when one chap buried an axe in another man's groin with tremendous force. I couldn't believe my eyes. For a minute I thought I was seeing my first Snuff movie.'

Benny had to be desperately offended to go even that far. It was not his nature to criticize even the world's worst performer. Whatever he thought in private, he would never speak out in public. He used to say: 'There are quite enough critics in our business. There are all the newspapers and magazines and the radio shows, and it sometimes seems like there are as many TV shows criticizing TV shows as there are TV shows. The last thing you should ever do in our business is criticize a fellow artist.'

But if Ben Elton failed to appreciate or begin to understand the basis of Benny Hill's comedy, the same was certainly not the case the other way around. Benny loved modern comics. He thought some of what is described as new wave comedy is brilliant. But he didn't like the really smutty stuff. And what confused him was that, while he was under attack for being a dirty old man, he was just naughty or a bit saucy while a lot of the modern comics were plain filthy. Once he watched a famous American comic on a TV show put out very late at night here, and he counted the obscenities. 'I counted seventy-six "mother-f———s" in an hour,' he said. 'Yet I remark that her dumplings are boiling over, and they say I am too dirty!'

One thing Benny couldn't understand was that kind of bad language in comedy. Not because it offended him, but because he believed that if you were going to use a four-letter word you should use it in the right place and not just throw it in for the sake of it. He thought the nine o'clock watershed in British TV, after which much raunchier material is allowed, was a nonsense. 'The difference between entertainment and filth is nine o'clock,' he said. 'Before nine o'clock tits is a dirty word. After nine o'clock you can say anything you like.'

About the strongest word Ben ever used on air was 'pillock' – and I think he invented its use as an insult. Ben loved words that sounded dirty but actually weren't. He originally had no idea what the word meant, but when he looked it up in a dictionary he found that it suited him perfectly. For knights in armour, a pillock was the medieval equivalent of a cricketer's or footballer's box. A very important piece of equipment.

Perhaps the funniest criticism Ben ever received was from the *Sun* newspaper, that well-known British bastion of good taste and restraint most famous for its daily offering of topless pin-ups on Page Three. In February 1981, under the headline 'Ban It, Benny!', the *Sun* published a wonderfully self-righteous leader article criticizing Benny and the show:

. . . Luscious ladies littered his show last Wednesday – and, on the face
of it, there was no need for complaint. But most of the views were
not of their faces. Exactly the opposite, in fact.

Benny has always been associated with cheek, but he really does not
need so much of this kind in his shows. Some of the shots were
downright kinky. The show is put out at a time to catch the family
audience, but Benny seems intent on appealing only to the dirty-
raincoat brigade.

Benny is a funny man and should steer away from the sort of show that
looks like a naughty underwear catalogue snapped through a hole
in the floor.

Ben was puzzled. 'It is the *Sun* that has the Page Three girls, isn't
it, Den?' he asked.

'Yes, Ben, it is.'

'Mmmm. Do you think they're jealous?' he chuckled.

The *Sun* leader genuinely amused Ben. Less amusing were the
comments made just a week after his death by Judge Pickles in his
column in the *Sun*.

'I am sorry about Benny Hill, and I know we should not speak ill
of the dead, but I am going to,' Pickles wrote. 'There should be more
humour than smirk and smut. But he never managed it. Though they
could have done it more tactfully, Thames TV were right to sack
him. He has since made millions abroad. That shows how superior
our humour is to theirs.'

But then, Judge Pickles was never a very good judge of anything, was he?

Ben always took any kind of criticism very seriously – too
seriously for his own good, I sometimes thought. He was badly hurt
by the sexist criticism, which he always felt was unfair. And a remark
which probably influenced him more than anything else was made by
the legendary American film-maker Hal Roach. Hal, one of the
original fathers of Hollywood and at the time of writing still alive and
nearly a hundred years old, was the producer of all the Laurel and

Hardy films. Asked while delivering a major university lecture if he believed any modern comic lived up to the comic geniuses of the past, notably Chaplin, Hal replied: 'I guess there is only one – Benny Hill. But I wish he'd clean up his act.'

It was a back-handed compliment from the great man, really, but none the less Ben had an intense rethink about his work. In the mid-eighties he did cut down on the sexier side of the show. There were fewer stocking tops and flashes of boob. But the image of *The Benny Hill Show* was always going to be stronger than the actuality. The feminist groups and the Ben Eltons of this world continued to see what was not there.

It was no accident, I feel, that we very rarely got letters of complaint from viewers. All correspondence was meticulously answered, and I do remember once getting a letter from a lady who objected strongly to what she referred to as a rape scene. Benny and I got the tapes out and took this show apart, because he was so worried by what this lady had seen in it. But in the end we just could not understand it. We could not see anything in it which could have been misconstrued in that way, and so we wrote back and asked the lady if she could explain exactly what it was that offended her. We never heard from her again.

Funnily enough, in twenty years with Thames TV Benny Hill was censored just once by the management, and that was over a scene with a dog. Nothing to do with sex at all. We hung a dog, and in a country like ours Thames reckoned that would never do. The scene was cut out, which was a great shame because Benny and I thought it was very funny. We had a dog on a lead and we hooked his lead on to a garage door while Benny was picking up a parcel. It was an electric door. Benny's wife drove over the button, the door swung open and the dog – by this time switched to a prop dog, a dummy, I must quickly point out – went right up in the air and hanged itself. As with so many of Benny's gags, it was based on a true story which he had read in a newspaper.

We recorded the scene in front of the studio audience and we knew it wasn't just us who found it funny. The audience roared. They loved it. But the boss said no. I remember saying: 'I suppose it would have been all right if we had hung little Jackie Wright.'

'Probably – but not a dog. Oh, no,' came the reply.

That was the only expression of dissatisfaction from Thames in all those years. What with that and producing a top rating show at home which sold to a hundred countries worldwide, no wonder we were a bit surprised to get the chop.

FOURTEEN

ONLY
A DREAM

The few months before he died were some of the best in Benny Hill's professional life. After three years in the TV wilderness, thanks to his extraordinary sacking, he was on the way back with a vengeance.

The TV companies had been fighting over him again. Days before his death, Benny struck a deal with Central to make a brand new series of *The Benny Hill Show*. He had agreed to put together three hour-long programmes. This time the contract had been thrashed out by his agent Linda Ronan, Richard Stones' partner, as Richard, now over seventy, is more or less retired. Benny never actually got to sign the contract. Poignantly, it was in the post when he died and arrived at his Teddington flat the day after his body was found.

The Central deal came after discussions with two other major TV companies. They were Carlton, about to take over the London weekday franchise from Thames, and Thames TV itself, now without a franchise to broadcast in the future but currently setting itself up as a major independent. Now Benny was a kindly and gentle man, not given to undue gloating or crowing, but he was tickled pink that Thames were now chasing him, just three years after showing him the door. He got a considerable amount of thoroughly understandable satisfaction out of the situation and was chuckling merrily when he phoned to tell me the news. 'Guess what, our kid . . . ,' he said.

Already Thames had asked if I could edit out a series of half-hours from his hour-long shows which, ironically were being trans-mitted when Benny died. But to be asked to make a whole new series of them was something else. Benny was extremely smiley about it. I cannot say he did not have an ego about his work. How could he not, when he loved his work so much?

I may never have understood why Thames TV sacked Ben but I sure as hell understood why they wanted him back. It was because of worldwide pressure. There were over a hundred countries hammering on the door of Thames International asking for more *Benny Hill Shows*, and there weren't any more left. The left hand selling programmes internationally at Thames had finally made contact with the right hand making the programmes, and the message was clear: 'We must have some new *Benny Hill Shows* because they are making us a fortune.' Benny knew exactly what was happening. He was very astute. And I suspect it gave him even more of a feeling of smiley satisfaction when we decided to turn the Thames offer down.

This was not done out of any sense of sour grapes. Far from it. Benny evaluated all three offers carefully. Thames remains a powerful organization, even without a broadcasting franchise, and will no doubt become an important TV production company. None the less, Thames have lost their shop window. If they made the shows, they would then have to sell them to a company with a franchise before they could be televised in Britain.

Carlton have gained a shop window, but have announced that they plan to be a TV publisher and not a broadcaster. In other words, they do not intend to set up a studio in which they will make programmes of their own – they will not be a production company.

Instead, they will either buy in programmes or finance independents to make programmes especially for them. So if Benny had accepted Carlton's offer it would not have been a complete package in the way he was used to. He would have made a deal with a major TV company and then have had to go to Fred Nerk Independent to have it made.

This left Central who, as has been well documented, had won their franchise in that crazy auction in 1991 with a bid of just £2000. So Central had retained their licence to broadcast, through succeeding with such a small bid had become probably the most financially stable of all the TV companies, and still had the kind of traditional studio system producing their own programmes with which Benny knew he would feel safest and most secure. That was why Benny decided to do a deal with Central. It is a tragedy that he did not live to work again on British TV, and a tragedy of almost equal proportion that he had been kept off the air in Britain for so long while at the same time conquering the rest of the world with devastating ease.

Ironically, Central TV had also come to an agreement with the other great comic who died at Easter 1992 – Frankie Howerd. Frankie had signed a contract with them for six half-hour comedy shows called *Frankie's On . . .*, in which he would perform solo in different situations. The first was *Frankie's On Board the Ark Royal*, in which Frankie entertained sailors aboard the famous aircraft carrier. Frankie had completed four of these programmes – all of which have been screened – when he died.

The new shows Benny was planning for Central were to have been classic Benny Hill, sticking fairly closely to the tried and tested formula. There would have been plenty of Fred Scuttle and the Chinaman and all the old favourites, but he was also devising new characters and planning to expand one or two things we had just touched on in the past which he rather liked and felt could be developed.

The usual team had, of course, already been told to expect to start work soon on a new series of *Benny Hill Shows*. Anna Dawson, Henry McGee, Bob Todd and Jon Jon Keefe were all to be part of the new line-up, along with Sue Upton and Louise English. Says Henry: 'The new shows had been under discussion for some time and Ben phoned me to tell me that he had done a deal with Central. We were all ready to go and looking forward to another series.' And so Ben's death was a double blow for the regular cast members of his show. The promise of steady work for some years to come died with him. And in the uncertain world of showbusiness that kind of news comes hard.

It's sad to think that all the material Ben had been compiling over the last few years will probably die with him also. Because who else could make it work? Ben's stuff was always so idiosyncratically his. There was loads of material lying around his flat when he died. He was a steady worker, producing ideas and writing constantly. The basic concept was often the same. He would take something quite ordinary and give it a twist. Films from when he was a boy gave him a wealth of inspiration. When he was in the army he got the idea of transposing the standard boy-meets-girl situation in a way which features in so much of his work.

'As a young soldier I would chat up a girl in the park who would turn me down and might say something like: " I don't believe in doing that sort of thing until you are married," ' he told me. 'It was while doing guard duty and just letting my mind wander that it occurred to me how silly that would sound coming from a man.'

So from the basic thought Ben developed a host of sketches over the years. From the thriller movie *The Collector*, in which a girl is kept prisoner by a man, Ben came up with a number in which the man is kept prisoner by a woman. Classic Benny Hill. And the film *Baby Doll* became the sketch 'Baby Boy'.

The Central series was to include its share of transposed male and female situations and a lot of material drawn from films and TV. We had been talking about basing a big sketch on Agatha Christie's *Poirot* and *Miss Marple* TV series – to be called 'Miss Marbles' – in which Benny would play both famous detectives. We reckoned we could have a lot of fun with the obsession with detail exercised by both of them. Imagine Benny as Miss Marple – played by Joan

Above. Ben and a cast of thousands.

Left. A dream come true. It was only a sketch but Ben's real life dream would have been much the same. *(Scope Features)*

Above. There is nothing like a Dame. Ben with pantomime stars Rula Lenska and Bernard Cribbins.

Right. I suppose a lick is out of the question? Ben is more interested in the real ice cream than rap star Vanilla Ice. (*Barry Brecken*)

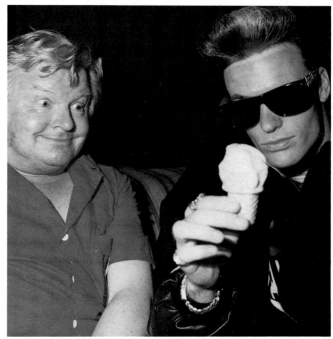

Above: Benny thanks my co-author, Hilary Bonner, for paying the lunch bill.

Left. Ben and I at the world's most famous recording studios. We're the ones with the halos. (*Scope Features*)

Top. Tea for four. My daughter
Joanna, aged six, Jade Westbrooke
and Sue Upton's son Richard with
Ben. *(Barry Brecken)*

Above. Ben keeping mum – with
young mums Sue Upton, Libby
Roberts and Jenny Westbrooke.
(Barry Brecken)

Right. And who is the biggest kid of
them all? One of the many
children's parties Ben gave,
especially on his birthdays. *(Scope
Features)*

Above. Just like Fred Scuttle, Michael Jackson salutes his hero, when he came to see Benny in hospital. *(Scope Features)*

Left. Doesn't he look well? I take Ben out for a walk during his second hospital stay. Sadly he wasn't as fit as he looked. *(Barry Brecken)*

Above. Ben raises a glass. Is that really orange juice: (*Scope Features*)

Left. Ben at home with the loves of his life: his TVs and video recorders. (*Scope Features*)

Below left. Benny not true to type. Scribbled notes were more his style. (*Scope Features*)

Above. Benny's last home – the riverside block in Teddington, Middlesex, where he rented a flat. (*Sunday Mirror*)

Below. Straight out of *Good Housekeeping*. But who on earth cleaned up the kitchen? (*Scope Features*)

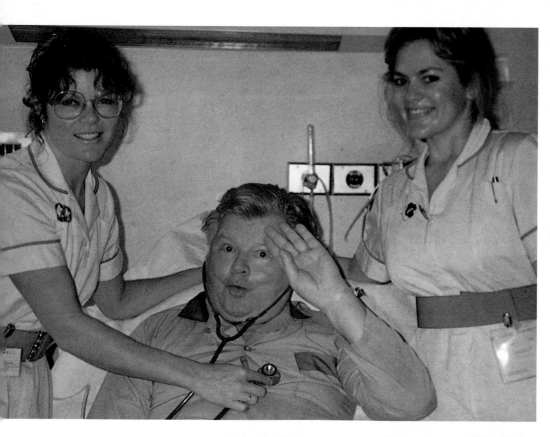

Above. Trust Ben to find two lovely angels – even in hospital. *(Scope Features)*

Right. At Ben's funeral, this elaborate wreath came from his close friend, Phoebe King, whom he called 'Kitten'. *(Daily Mirror)*

To Teddy Bear,
I love you very
very much,
Kitten. [Phoebe]

Hickson in the hit BBC series – fussing about which side of the saucer the teaspoon was placed or which hand was holding the piece of cake, while people are being hacked to pieces and shot and bodies are falling out of cupboards all over the place. Ben particularly loved David Suchet's portrayal of Poirot and could not wait to do a micky-take of it. He was already rehearsing his bad Belgian accent and preparing to mix up all the words, as he did so well.

As ever with Ben, writing his comedy was a continual jotting down of notes and playing with ideas rather than one concerted effort. He did not announce that he was starting work and sit down and concentratedly write in a big chunk when a show was imminent.

He never stopped working in his own particular way. He used to say that if he wrote just thirty seconds of material every day that was three TV hours – fifty-two minutes each – a year. He didn't need a particular project to be looming, he just carried on with his own routine. On the basis of this a newspaper reporter obviously desperate for a new line, referred to Benny having the cushiest job in showbiz. After all, thirty seconds' work a day – what's that? Cushy, of course.

None the less, I was always quite sure that if at any time at all I had said: 'Right, Benny. We've been given this slot. We have to start filming a new show next week. When can we talk props?' it would never have been a problem. Benny always had more than enough material up his sleeve.

And although he was shattered when he was sacked by Thames, it didn't stop him from carrying on writing in his usual way. In his mind there would be little or no connection between the two. One of the most common effects that being sacked or being made redundant can have on very able people is that they are so shocked they become incapable of doing anything for a while. Benny wasn't affected in that way at all. Work was, after all, a way of life for him and it did not change.

During those wilderness years Ben made one hour-long show for American TV. It was called *The World of Benny Hill* and was the only one he ever did specifically for a foreign market. And, ironically, we filmed it at Thames TV Studios at Teddington. The reason was simple. They were the cheapest studios to hire at the time. Some of the location work was done in America and some in Europe. As well as the inevitable old favourites like Fred Scuttle, Ben introduced new American-orientated characters. The show included impersonations of Roseanne Barre and sex therapist Dr Ruth.

Ben made this show for Don Taffner, who had always handled foreign sales for Thames TV and is now one of the biggest independent producers and distributors in the States. It was a great confidence booster for Benny. 'The break-up with Thames was bound to knock my confidence,' he said at the time. 'But within days Don was on the phone from New York saying his company wanted to sign me up. I owe all my success in America to Don. He sold my shows on their stations and made them want me.' Don never lost faith in Ben. Why should he? Better than anybody else, probably, he recognized the enormity of Ben's status in America. After all, Don still handled the distribution for all Benny's shows and he knew just how huge the market was. So Ben kept his hand in – although, sadly, Taffner failed to raise the finance needed to make several more *Benny Hill Shows* as he had originally planned.

Ben was so rich that the money from his immense overseas sales had probably ceased to mean a lot by the end. But the worldwide adulation he received meant everything to him during what would otherwise have been a very bleak time. It helped him to maintain the certainty that he would return to British TV, which he so terribly desired. His sense of humour, too, helped him keep a sense of proportion about it all.

It was during this period that he began an association with the Hawaiian Tropic sun oil people, which led to him advertising their products on TV and judging their annual competitions in their home base of Daytona, Florida, and in the Bahamas. Who could be better suited to such a job than Ben? And this particular deal enabled him to pursue his favourite occupation of taking working holidays in glamorous locations.

Wherever we were, if conversation touched on his popularity Benny would go into the same routine. 'Do you know, Den, we are in Madrid and it is four o'clock in the afternoon. And you can guarantee that at this very moment and at any moment of every single day, at any given time, somebody somewhere in the world is watching one of my shows and saying, "What a load of crap!"' He may well have been right. But also, during those British wilderness years, stories kept rolling in from all over the world about the response to Benny's shows, which brought a chuckle or two into the despondency he fought so hard to keep at bay.

In most parts of America Ben's shows used to be broadcast between 11 and 11.30 pm. And a change in lights-out time at a famous American prison caused a riot – all because of Ben. Prisoners at the grim San José Penitentiary in California created hell when they were told that their bedtime had been brought forward half an hour to 11 pm. This meant they could no longer watch *The Benny Hill Show*. They went potty. They set fire to their beds, blocked the lavatories with newspapers and blankets, and threw any unattached items of furniture out the windows. The place was awash with sewage and cinders. As Ben said to me at the time: 'I know there is really nothing funny about a prison riot – but what a reason! All that because they couldn't see *The Benny Hill Show*. You can't help just a little chuckle, can you?'

Some years earlier, we had learned of an incident which brought home just how important Benny appeared to be even in times of extreme crisis. During the Falklands War we were sent a copy of the Argentinian equivalent of *TV Times*, which featured on the cover a picture of Benny with his girls. This was at a time when Argentinian and British servicemen were dying in action. Benny was astonished.

'Doesn't this bring home the nonsense of it all?' Benny asked me. 'Here I am, a British comic on the front of an Argentinian magazine when we are at war with each other. Wouldn't it be better if we solved our problems with laughter and humour instead of guns?'

The demand for Benny Hill in America was and remains staggering. In 1990 Ben discussed a £5 million offer to star in an American film about a burlesque house, and a £6 million offer to make twenty-six half-hour shows for American TV. He turned both down. He never liked to be involved in anything which he felt he couldn't control. He did not feel the film was right for him, and he did not like the idea of making so many half-hour shows. He liked his usual hour-long format, and he did not feel he did his best work under pressure. And he certainly did not need the money, which continues to roll in even after his death. Already a re-release of his hit record 'Ernie: The Fastest Milkman in the West', has bounced back into the charts, causing one determinedly trendy disc jockey to walk off his Radio One show in disgust.

Benny rarely put a professional foot wrong, and he was always appreciated abroad even when that was not the case at home. He loved any kind of recognition from the British establishment, which probably stems from his upbringing and that overblown respect for any kind of authority which I have talked about earlier.

He was overjoyed when, just six months before his death, he was invited to a reception at the British Embassy in Paris by the Ambassador, Sir Ewen Fergusson – he and his family turned out to be great fans. Benny was taken on a guided tour of the Embassy, which contains a room housing the four-poster bed belonging to Pauline Borghese, daughter of Napoleon. He was in his element, and particularly pleased because he was accompanied by the camera crew making the *Omnibus* documentary about him for BBC TV. So his moment of official glory was to be permanently recorded.

'This is the first time I have ever been invited to a British Embassy anywhere,' he said. And I swear there were tears in his eyes.

I always felt Ben did not get the recognition he deserved at home, although he never mentioned it. But he must have been aware of the long list of so much lesser people in showbusiness who were awarded MBEs and OBEs and even knighthoods in his lifetime.

Benny, Britain's greatest showbusiness envoy overseas in history, got nothing at all.

Most of all, he sorely missed his British TV showcase. Had he lived to fulfill that contract with Central and return to British television in style that would have fulfilled his final dream. It was not to be. And the irony surrounding his wilderness years was further emphasized when right after his death Thames TV – the station which dumped him – broadcast a glowing tribute to Ben. They built it around one of the half-hour specials I had edited for them for screening this year.

Of course, by then Thames already knew they had lost their franchise. It was just two years after Ben's sacking that they lost their licence to broadcast. Ben took no pleasure in that – he had too many friends at Thames – but he did recognize the pathos. Perhaps there is indeed a comic in the sky somewhere who watched out for Ben – if so, I hope he's still watching out for him.

OBSESSIONS

Food was, without doubt, the great love of Benny Hill's life. It was also his torture. And his eating and dieting habits may have contributed to the heart disease which ultimately killed him. He was a binge eater. So he took appetite-depressant drugs and would diet strictly, eating very little for days on end and drinking only low-calorie soft drinks. Then he would break out and stuff himself with food washed down with wine and brandy.

Those famous photographs of a sad-looking Benny Hill carting home carrier bags full of food were emblazoned across every newspaper in the land. Benny was outraged. 'How else am I supposed to get my shopping home?' he asked. He loved shopping, and above all he liked buying food. And if he looked sad and downtrodden it was probably because he had behaved himself in his local supermarket and the carrier bags did not contain the forbidden goodies he so adored, particularly sweet things like gooey cream cakes and boxes of rich chocolates.

Benny had a saying about food. It was simple and to the point.

'There is,' he would proclaim, 'no such thing as bad food.' He adored eating. He adored Chinese food, Italian food, French food, English food, food from all over the world. Anything at all, as long as there was lashings of it.

Yet, at least in his last days, he knew that his excessive eating habits could kill him. He must try to cut down and lose weight. Every day of his life, 365 days a year, Benny was desperately trying to stick to some kind of diet. He was permanently overweight, yet counting calories was almost an obsession with him. He knew the calorie count of almost everything on the supermarket shelf. He knew how many calories there were in a chocolate Smartie, did Ben. Every day he would attempt to be frugal. Toast for breakfast. Low-calorie drinks. Ham and salad for lunch. Maybe cereal in the evening.

He went shopping frequently, sometimes two or three times a day. Because his one hope of sticking to any kind of diet control was quite simply to have in the house only what he planned to eat for the next meal. If he bought a packet of chocolate biscuits he would not stop until he had eaten all of them. If he bought six cans of soup he would open them all and eat the lot, probably with mountains of bread and butter. If he bought enough meat and veg for two days he would devour it all in one go. He would get through an entire loaf of bread smothered with butter and jam, and if there was still some jam left at the end he would finish it off on the remains of the biscuits or eat it by the spoonful until it was gone.

His calorie obsession was what led to newspaper reports about this multimillionaire spending hours in supermarkets checking prices. He was actually peering painstakingly at everything he bought to check the calorie count. And that was something he did every day of his life. He also used to check the fat content of various foods to such an extent that he once lamented: 'If there was low-fat fat, that's what I would have.'

He dealt with drinking too much in the same way that he dealt with eating too much. Benny loved a drink, but he never kept alcohol in the house. It never stayed long enough. If Benny had a bottle of brandy at home he would keep drinking it until it was finished. So usually the only drinks he took home were low-calorie soft ones.

If somebody was coming he would go out and buy two bottles of champagne, or if they liked vodka or sherry or whatever he would buy a bottle of that. He'd sometimes buy some white wine if I was going round, because he knew that was my drink. I'd have a glass and then we would maybe have to go out, but we never actually went out until that bottle was empty. And if he got vodka in for someone he would finish that before the end of the day too, I know. It was not because he was a drunk. He was a glutton. If he could get his hands on food or drink he could not resist.

In spite of all his efforts he was permanently overweight, and yet he was desperately vain about his weight. His whole family were big, plump people. Benny weighed 16½ stone. His brother Leonard weighed 23½ stone when he died, and he was shorter than Ben's five foot nine-ish. The whole world knew him as a chubby comic, good old round-faced, giggly Ben. But Benny never came to terms with it. And every time he watched one of his shows, there he was, at least three sizes bigger than he should be. He so wanted to be a male Twiggy.

It was not possible, partly because of the way he was made and partly because of his love of food. Periods of near starvation were invariably followed by those destructive binges. He also did dreadful things to himself in bids to beat his weight problem. He took those awful appetite-depressant things, and he damn near overdosed on them. I didn't realize what he was doing for a long time, and then it all began to make sense.

He was popping these prescribed amphetamines – speed. While they were depressing his appetite they were also speeding things up. We used to be away on a location early in the morning and there would be Benny running at 400 mph. You didn't have to shoot him at six frames for our trick scenes – he was already going at double speed anyway. At seven o'clock in the morning in the middle of a wet field I would have a spinning top on my hands. Then when the things wore off he would come down, and that could be even worse.

Now this was in my early years directing *The Benny Hill Show*, and although I knew that something was up it was not until long afterwards that I understood what it was. He really tucked into those pills when we were filming, because location catering is so wonderful and tempting. It can turn even thin men into fatties. The standard is always so high – out of these tacky little vans come delicious gourmet meals, and they feed you every five minutes or thereabouts. It is difficult for anyone not to eat far too much, let alone a dedicated foodie like Benny. I think that's why he invented the run-off in his shows in a bid to get some weight off through being chased everywhere.

First thing in the morning when Ben arrived on set he would be greeted with the sight of the crew all tucking into these lovely double egg and bacon breakfasts, fried potatoes and fried bread on the side, mushrooms, beans, sausages, toast and butter, coffee with cream – anything you wanted. Irresistible to Ben. As I think about it now I can see his face, eyes damp with longing, damn near drivelling at the sight of mounds of that kind of food. And so before he left home in the mornings Benny would start taking these pills, so that he had at least some control and would try not to eat until lunchtime.

When I did find out what had been going on I was very upset with him. I knew the dangers. And when he had to have a kidney removed in 1976 I always reckoned the amphetamines he took might have contributed to that. I am no doctor, but I know that they affect liquid retention and that means they must affect the kidneys.

Benny had a tumour on his kidney which turned out to be benign. Typically, he did his best to turn the episode into a joke. 'It was benign, you know – it used to smile a lot,' he said.

Henry McGee visited Benny in hospital and remembers how hard Benny tried to be funny. 'I went along knowing that I should not overtire him, and he made me laugh so much I was worn out when I left the hospital,' he recalls. 'I'm sure all that effort stemmed from his basic shyness. He knew how awkward *he* would feel making a hospital visit, so he worked overtime to make you feel at ease. And the only way he knew was through humour.'

But in reality the operation was no joke. If you lose an organ like a kidney it puts extra strain on the heart to make the other kidney work overtime. So who knows what harm Benny did himself with his dieting fads?

He also had the binge eater's habit of trying to kid not only other people but probably also himself that he was not eating as much as he actually was.

When we had a tea break during filming there would be trays of tea and biscuits and cakes brought out. I would be standing talking to Ben and suddenly he would disappear. He would be thirty yards away or something, standing alone in a field with his back to everyone. And no, this was not an example of Benny Hill the loner. This, I am afraid, was Benny Hill the compulsive eater. What he used to do was grab a big handful of chocolate biscuits or cakes and then stroll around looking as if he was thinking about something while somehow contriving to eat all his booty secretly.

When he returned, it used to amuse me mildly to ask him if he would like a biscuit. He was always quite convinced that nobody noticed what he was doing and, having actually consumed ten or so, he would say innocently: 'Oh, no, nothing for me, little heart.'

But he did understand his own weaknesses. And that was why he was so strict with himself when he went shopping, which he enjoyed more than almost anyone I have ever known. He adored supermarkets. Far from studying prices and counting the cost, Benny was actually embarrassed to be seen spending small amounts. If we went into a chemist's together and all Ben wanted was a packet of razor blades costing a few pence he would also buy a bottle of aftershave for thirty quid or so. And then he would ask if I wanted some aftershave.

'Oh, go on, have some. Have a big bottle,' he would say.

Now everyone likes aftershave. But not that much. Ben was just embarrassed about putting down just a pound or two on the counter. He didn't want people saying that he came into their shop and only spent so much. The publicity about his alleged meanness really bothered him, so he used to go the other way to make sure nobody could possibly think it was true.

And so he might spend ages in the supermarket dithering on which size of his favourite fish fingers to buy for his supper, the sensible small one or the big one, and then, in order to save face, he would buy something wildly expensive that he didn't need and usually shouldn't have.

For Benny eating out was a huge treat, and the calorie counting invariably went out the window. He used to go right through the card, and pudding trolleys were his greatest passion of all. If he went out to dinner and went totally over the top he would then starve himself for two days.

His weight was always on his mind. He would mutter to himself while ordering a meal. 'I shouldn't really,' he would say as his eye was attracted to something really gooey and delicious. 'I have plenty of will power but not a lot of won't power,' was one of his lines when talking about food.

He was actually quite a good cook, and in his younger days used occasionally to entertain quite lavishly at his Queens Gate apartment. At that time, if he was entertaining a girl he might cook for her. I don't think he ever cooked anything elaborate just for himself, and in latter years, as he became more and more reluctant to invite people into his home, he rarely cooked proper meals at all. Apart from any other considerations, cooking would have meant stocking up the fridge and that would bring with it too much temptation.

Eating was a sensual pleasure for Benny and he had rather odd little habits. He never mixed different tastes, and always ate every part of a meal separately. If he had a plate full of steak, chips, mushrooms and peas, first he ate the steak, then the chips, then the mushrooms and finally the peas. He would never put a little bit of everything on his fork and eat it all in one mouthful.

And if he drank wine with a meal he would not sip it as he ate. He would stop eating for a moment, pick up his wineglass and drain it in one big swallow, and then go back to eating until he felt like another drink. At that point he would refill his glass and go through the same procedure.

He loved to experiment with food and he liked surprises. On the rare occasions when there was something on a menu in a foreign language that he did not understand he would say: 'I know what everything is on the menu except that dish. So that is the one I am going to have.'

His capacity when he gave in to temptation and went on a binge was daunting. I have only once seen him beaten. Benny and I were in New York and we went for a walk in Chinatown, where we decided to have lunch. It was a Saturday and the place was packed with Chinese families all eating out, but eventually we found a restaurant that had room for us. We were seated at a big round table along with some Chinese people and given a couple of menus, and it was like a day off for Benny because nobody recognized him in Chinatown – about the only place in New York you could ever say that about.

We asked for a couple of Tiger beers and then started to order the meal. We picked five or six dishes to share, the way you do in England, one sweet and sour pork, one chicken with bamboo shoots, one special fried rice . . . and so on. This lovely old gentleman who was writing out our order in the most beautiful Chinese began to look more and more puzzled. Eventually he began pointing at all the dishes on the menu that we had chosen. 'You wan' that one? And that one? And that one . . . ?'

'Yeah, yeah,' we said.

Off he went, and then another, younger waiter came over and went through the same puzzled routine, carefully checking our order.

Off he went and a third man came over, and we went through it all again. By this time we had a pretty fair idea that we had done something wrong, but we didn't know what it was.

'Perhaps they've recognized you,' I said to Ben.

'I don't think so,' he replied slowly.

We found out soon enough. The other people on our table were all smiling at us a lot, and then they started clearing away their beer cans and their plates and making a lot of room.

At last a waiter arrived, staggering under the weight of the biggest dish you had ever seen – piled a foot high. And that was just the rice. Every item on the menu that we had ordered was that size. It seemed that in this restaurant each dish you ordered was for a family of eight – and we two idiot Englishman had ordered six of them. We tried to play it cool at first. No problems. We rolled up our sleeves and dug in.

But forty-two large portions of Chinese food proved to be too much even for a man of Benny's gargantuan capacity. So we gave most of the food away to other tables. It was the prices that had totally confused us, I think. This restaurant had to be the best bargain in New York. Our bill for all this food was about 25 dollars or something ridiculous. Ben paid, as usual, and knowing him the tip he left was probably more than the cost of the meal.

Being aware that he could afford to eat in any restaurant anywhere in the world as often as he liked probably increased Benny's torment over food. He was perpetually torn between his desire to eat and his desire to fight the flab. When he came out of hospital after his heart attack Benny knew that he was in serious trouble and had to do what he was told by the doctors. And of course, they wanted him to lose weight. They didn't put him on any kind of special diet, which I think may have been because they knew he would cheat. They told him the good things and the bad things to eat – which he knew already, although it rarely stopped him – and said he should lose two pounds a month. Not a lot. They didn't want him to do anything drastic.

He began really losing weight for the first time since I had met him. I think he had been frightened, so he made a real effort. He always had that lovely chubby round face without a wrinkle on it, and you could see in his face that he was losing weight. Strangely enough, it didn't suit him. His chin started to get scraggy. He was aware of that and didn't like it. 'We're going to have to have some high-heeled shirts built, young Den,' he said. That chubby face had always given him an agelessness. And of course the shock of grey hair, which looked blond when lit for the camera, added to the illusion of youth.

It was a rather bad joke, for me at any rate, that when I first met Ben as a floor manager on his show he told me that he was worried about losing his hair. I remember saying: 'What? Can you see your eyebrows?' And although I was a lot younger than Ben my hair had seriously thinned out by the time he died, while he still had the same beautiful unruly thatch.

He did not change much facially in all the time that I knew him. But the paunch grew gradually bigger as he grew older, in the way that paunches do.

SIXTEEN

SUPERTRAVEL

Ben was the eternal traveller. And when he travelled he did it in style. He took me with him all over the world, sometimes when we were working together doing promotions for *The Benny Hill Show*, and sometimes just for the hell of it. He adored everything about travel, from the sensation of being on the move, of going somewhere new, to the joy of staying in luxurious hotels. The novelty never wore off. It suited Benny perfectly to be able to press a buzzer and know that a big juicy steak and a bottle of champagne would just arrive. No opening the fridge and discovering you were out of eggs.

And for Ben there was always the added thrill of the mass adulation he attracted in every new town. It was seductive – you could get hooked on it like a drug. Benny would have had to be a saint – which he certainly wasn't – not to revel in it. And I found that I quickly began to bask in the reflected glory.

While there seemed to be times in Britain when sniping at Benny became a national pastime, the adoration he got abroad was constant and sensational. You just became used to him being mobbed wherever he went, and grew to expect it. All over Europe and in America he was adored, and the people went mad when they recognized him wherever he went. Almost always when we went abroad Ben was mobbed.

His popularity at home has never really been in doubt, in spite of that crazy Thames sacking and the rantings of various feminist groups who never understood what he was about. But when Ben was recognized in the street in the UK he would be hailed as an old friend, maybe, or just stared at. Yes, he would frequently be asked for autographs. But he did not find himself unable to move in the streets because he was surrounded by crowds of people screaming for him. In America and in many parts of Europe Bennymania was rampant, and it was quite an experience. You could be caught out, though. With a bit of luck there is always something in life to bring the biggest of stars down to earth.

When we travelled to that Cannes TV Festival, we arrived at Nice Airport to find total chaos. The car which was supposed to pick us up had not arrived, and while we were looking around and trying to find out what was happening Bennymania struck with a vengeance. Within seconds our Ben was surrounded by about fifty people all wanting to touch him, to talk to him, to get his autograph. They were enthusiastic and demanding, and I began to think that I must get him away from all of this before it got out of hand. 'Come on, we'll just have to get a cab,' I said. Somehow I managed to get all these punters off him and whisk him outside, where there was a howling gale blowing. The trees were bending, there was rubbish everywhere blowing around, waste bins and flower pots hurtling about like missiles in a war zone.

Suddenly, salvation. There was this little old guy standing calmly smiling at us. He was a cab driver and he loaded us into his taxi and we set off thankfully for Cannes. Half of Benny's fan club had followed us outside and they were all waving and cheering. Then this guy turned around, still grinning, and said: 'Meester 'Ill!'

'Yeah, yeah,' I said. Benny and I just wanted to get to our hotel. Now we had to deal with another adoring fan all the way to Cannes. An unworthy response, but we were only human.

'Meester 'Ill,' our driver said again.

Benny was just sitting there quietly, not really wanting to get involved. 'Yeah, yeah,' I said. 'Meester 'Ill. We'll give you the photo and the autograph when we get to the hotel. Yeah.'

And I don't speak French.

Then he said 'Meester 'Ill' again just as we were driving along a boulevard of palm trees which were going crazy in the wind, and suddenly the truth dawned on Benny and me. The poor man didn't have a clue who Benny was. He was trying to say 'Mistral'.

Life was work, and work was life, for Benny. If he was required by Thames to do a bit of publicity somewhere he would agree to do all the photocalls and interviews required on condition that he had a complete day off before and a couple of days after. To him these kinds of trips were a perfect opportunity to go exploring. I became something of a minder to Benny on these occasions, because it really did get crazy and the mob scenes could be quite frightening.

Greece was the worst of all. The show was really huge there, and we agreed to go over on a promotional visit with some of the Hill's Angels. Two main events were planned: a press call at Athens airport and a photocall at the Acropolis.

The madness began as we coasted to a halt on the tarmac. I looked out of the window at an army of cameramen, film crews and reporters all standing on the edge of the runway waiting. Eventually we found enough courage to leave the plane and ran for the usual bus – from which we were promptly removed. There was this ruddy great Cadillac waiting to take us the fifty yards or so to the airport building. Everybody else went on the bus – but not Benny Hill. We gave a press conference in the first-class lounge and it was packed. 'Will it be like this wherever we go?' I asked. 'Oh, yes,' they said. And they were right.

In order to get us to our hotel we were given a police escort. There were four motorcycles in front of our car, four on either side, and four behind. Incredible. We hurtled through Athens at top speed, right through all the lights – it was terrifying.

I shouted to the driver: 'We'd rather meet the press than be dead!'

In spite of being weak with fear, Benny had not entirely lost his sense of humour. 'I wouldn't go as far as to say that,' he muttered.

The next day we were taken to the Acropolis, and I think we became the first people to be thrown off it since the Turkish invasion. I had got Benny dressed as a traditional Greek soldier in pom-pom shoes, little white skirt and red tights. The girls were in costume too.

It's a long walk up to the Acropolis from the place where all the cars have to park, and they bent the rules and took us up a little further. When we clambered out of our car the world went mad. There were about five hundred people there, Greeks and a lot of Americans, all crying: 'Benny, Benny, Benny!' It was sheer madness. Eventually the curator asked us to leave. I think he was afraid of what might happen, and I felt much the same. We had to go across the road to shoot the picture with the Acropolis in the background. All that fuss over this middle-aged plump chap with glasses.

But on occasions the manic adulation could be a great advantage. I was despatched to America once when *The Benny Hill Show* was up for an Emmy award. It was in the days when we could not get Benny himself to go to America. I was phoned up by Thames at the last moment and asked to travel to Los Angeles for the ceremony. It would have been the last minute, because without doubt one of the big bosses would have been down to go to a nice posh do like that and I was just a substitute.

Anyway, there was no way I was going to be proud about it. I was filming some other show at the time and I was pretty busy, so I handed my passport over to the travel people at Thames so that they would have all the details. They organized tickets, hotel, the lot and just handed me everything in an envelope.

I went to the airport, got on my plane and flew across the Atlantic. It was just before the Los Angeles Olympics and security was double-double. At the other end I collected my case and went to Immigration, where I presented my passport to a big uniformed guy sitting at a desk.

He opened it, flipped through it, flipped through it again, and said: 'Where is your visa?'

My heart stopped. 'I haven't got a visa,' I stammered.

'You haven't got one?' he said. He stood up and pushed himself back from the desk, undid the button on his gun holster at his waist and rested his hand, just lightly, on the gun handle.

'How did you get on the plane in England?' he asked.

'I just got on it,' I said.

'You just got on it,' he repeated. He pushed an alarm bell of some kind under the desk, and I looked behind me. There were cops with guns standing around us holding back the rest of the passengers on the flight.

The Immigration man picked up a phone. 'Hey, George, we've got a guy here just come off the BA flight and he hasn't got a visa. Yeah. I asked him how he got on the plane in England, George, and he said he just got on it. Yeah, George, I thought you might like to come up.'

Now I didn't have a visa because it was my first-ever trip to America and I didn't even know I needed one. Thames didn't even check, because they just assumed I had been to the States dozens of times and already had one.

And the reason I was not stopped at Heathrow, where visas were always checked on the way out in those days, was that the man who was supposed to look at my passport had been to see a *Benny Hill Show* being filmed just a couple of weeks before. He recognized me, started to chat, and I am pretty sure he didn't even open my passport. How do you begin to explain that?

I realized that I was in serious trouble. 'What happens next?' I asked nervously.

'We check you out. If you get lucky we lock you up until the next available flight to England, and then we send you home. That's if you get lucky. If we have any doubts about you – you go to jail.'

I started to jabber. 'But I can't go to jail! I've got all these people waiting for me, and I've got to go to the Emmy ceremony because my show's up for an award.'

His expression said quite clearly that he considered it fairly unlikely that anyone trying to get into America without a visa had a show up for an Emmy.

'Oh, yeah? And what show is that?' he asked languidly.

'I produce and direct *The Benny Hill Show*,' I said.

'Naw! You're kidding, you don't?' He was starting to grin. I couldn't believe it. 'You do what? Why, he's the greatest goddamn comic that was ever born.'

By this time George had arrived, accompanied by another guard called Bernard, and things were obviously looking up. But I wasn't entirely sure of myself so I resisted the urge to ask where Shaw was. They all started talking about Benny – and they really were called George and Bernard. It's the truth – I couldn't make it up. 'You direct his show? Aw, we love that guy. That guy is the best.' Suddenly they were all over me. The rest of the passengers were still being held back by cops with guns while my Immigration man started to get busy. He called for an eight-thirty-six form, or some such thing, passed it to me then said: 'Aw, Dennis, you don't need to fill it in. Look, you just sign at the bottom and I'll fill it in for you, OK?'

Within ten minutes I was in the country. Before the name of Benny Hill worked its magic I was about to be locked up. In those days you did not get into America without a visa. It did not happen. It was impossible. Unless, of course, you produced and directed Benny. Then anything was possible.

Thames cameraman Ted Adcock discovered the power of Benny Hill when he was in America working on a documentary about the Mafia. A Godfather character had refused to be interviewed on film – until he learned that Ted was Benny's regular cameraman. The Mafia chief then said that he would be filmed after all, as long as Ted told Benny that he must appear in the Mafia man's Las Vegas club.

Wherever and whenever Benny travelled he was all the while gathering material. Virtually every time he went into a restaurant to eat he would come out with some kind of routine on the waiter: the lazy waiter, the waiter in a hurry to get home, the snooty waiter.

A favourite was the posh menu sketch. Benny would be given the posh 100 franc menu, table beautifully laid, lovely glass and cutlery. But actually he wants the cheap 50 franc menu. He tells the waiter this. Off comes the tablecloth, the waiter throws the knives and forks at him, and so on.

After the Montreux TV Festival once Benny took me to Paris for a few days. He remembered that I had never been and just wanted to show me around. We booked in to the George V Hotel, and as usual Benny told me not to worry about money – he was going to pay for everything. This was just as well, because a few days at the George V would have meant another mortgage for me.

Ben knew Paris backwards and couldn't wait to show it off. 'We'll walk everywhere,' he said, which was fine by me because I liked walking almost as much as he did. But he did his trick of setting off at 100 miles an hour with his head down. He was rattling on and his little feet were going and neither of us was able to see anything. Finally I sat myself down at a café and he didn't even notice. He was talking to himself. Eventually he realized something was up, looked around and came rushing back. 'How long have you been Seb Coe?' I asked.

After that we started to stroll and could appreciate the sights. And he discovered the advantage that, at least on a private visit, if he was walking with me people did not necessarily barge in and mob him even when he was recognized. He began to relax a bit.

He was always overwhelmingly generous on these trips. He would give me a bunch of money and say: 'There you are, young Den. Now you do all the tipping.' But it was usually a little more than tipping money. Then he would have a go at me and tell me not to be stingy with it because he knew tipping always confused me. I have never understood why you have to tip the taxi driver and the hairdresser and not that smashing bloke in the shirt shop who really helped you out.

Benny, on the other hand, was ludicrous with his tips. At the Thames studio restaurant the prices used to be marvellous and Ben would leave the girls a twenty-quid tip for a six-quid meal – no wonder they all adored him. He was a bit stupid about it, really. He was determined that people should know he was a generous man, but he didn't have to do that – he *was* a generous man.

Once, when Benny was making *The Italian Job* with Michael Caine, he had a couple of days off and went on a train ride across Europe just for the hell of it. He had handfuls of currency for the different countries and when he stopped somewhere in France and went and had a meal he paid in Swiss francs by mistake. Benny had deliberately tried to leave his usual enormous tip, so when the restaurant boss told him he had paid far too much Benny just waved him away. It was only when he got back on a train again that he realized he had given them about £250 instead of £25.

Many years later he took a girl with him on the same train trip because he had enjoyed it so much. And he went back to that restaurant. They remembered him vividly. And not because he was Benny Hill. He described it to me as: 'Hey, here comes the mad Englishman. Now we'll be able to buy the pump for the bicycle.'

The first time I went abroad with Benny was when I was still the floor manager and John Robins was producer of *The Benny Hill Show*. Benny and I were already getting along like a house on fire, and one day he said to me: 'Right, nature boy. We're going to hit the town. You, me and John Robins are all going to Hamburg.'

At the last minute John dropped out and Benny and I went alone. I don't think Hamburg has ever recovered. We were like two schoolkids in a sweet shop. We went from bar to bar and restaurant to restaurant. Benny was not well known in Germany then, so he could do what he liked. We went to all the naughty clubs which make you giggle, because they are not sexy at all – or we didn't find them so, anyway. We went to the Reeperbahn, where all the call girls sit in windows plying their trade. 'There you go, our Den, have a good look around,' he said. He sat in the sunshine outside a bar with a newspaper – his favourite recreation – while I wandered about for a bit.

In another life Benny Hill could have been a tourist guide. Nothing gave him more joy than showing a newcomer around a town he loved. I was with Benny on my first visit to Madrid. As I walked into my hotel room the phone rang and Benny was on the other end, asking if I was ready to go out sightseeing.

'I've not even unpacked yet,' I said.

'Never mind that – I want to show you Madrid,' he replied.

He was like an excited kid again, so much so that he took me up in one of the cable cars that fly across the park, even though he was terrified of heights. Then we wandered around a fairground, which was half empty because we were out of season, just eating popcorn and looking around.

Soon he wanted to eat a proper meal, as Benny always did, and we went to this big open air restaurant with room for about five hundred people. Although it was virtually empty there was a rock group playing. They very quickly became aware that Benny was there. It was strange. One minute they were playing to twenty bored punters. The next they were entertaining the world's biggest come- dian. You could tell they were directing everything at him and he was loving it – always a good audience, was Benny.

Afterwards we went on a tube train. Benny had already had a few drinks and so he was talking to everyone. We visited several more bars and a flamenco club before Benny finally said rather uncertainly: 'I think I have had too much to drink.'

We took a cab, and when we got back to our hotel both of us could barely walk. We were feeling no pain. But as we staggered past reception Benny underwent a transformation. For a few minutes, as we picked up our room keys and when he knew everyone was looking at him, he somehow managed to appear sober as a judge. It was very impressive. That was the actor in him. Then we got in the lift and he virtually collapsed in a heap saying: 'Den, we'll never drink Fundador again . . .'

That was Ben on the toot. But he was usually a very discerning tourist – much more than a tourist really. He looked and listened and learned wherever he went. And this is where his tremendous skill with languages came in. Apart from being fluent in French, German and Spanish and pretty good at Italian and Greek, Benny could quickly pick up a smattering of the language wherever we went. He had an ear for it. And so when we travelled he used to buy all the local papers and read them avidly to find out exactly what was going on. He loved to turn up at a little village fete or a dance or a carnival or a fair miles from anywhere.

Once in Spain he whisked me off to a circus in a remote village. 'I've found out the train times so we'll go by train because it's much more fun, and then we'll get a cab back.' He loved to experience as much local colour as possible. And so we arrived at what was really little more than a tent show in a village. Inevitably he was recognized, and the people were amazed to see him. After the show he was invited into their caravans, where he told them how much he had enjoyed the show and was very gracious. He was always doing things like that. It was a little-known side of Benny and it made him a lot of friends. He liked having fun as much as the next man. It was just that he chose to do so in ways not normally associated with worldwide superstars.

He adored local customs. And he loved spectacles and spectacular showmanship, which probably explains his passion for bull-fighting – an enthusiasm I did not share. When in Spain he used to seek out the big bullfights and even plan his visits to coincide with them. I had a go at him about it once – the very idea of a bullfight makes me feel sick – and told him he should be ashamed of himself. I also told him that in any case he would have to stop going to them because if he was spotted there would be a terrific backlash.

'Most of your fans everywhere in the world except Spain would be shocked and disgusted to learn that you go to bullfights,' I told him. 'They would be really offended.'

'Would they, Den?' he said mildly. I don't think he ever gave a thought to the real unpalatable truth about bullfighting – he was just mesmerized by the excitement of it, the high drama. As much as anything he liked the small village fights where the local hero would go into the ring. Like everything he was interested in, he studied it meticulously. He knew all there was to know about bullfighting – the history, the tradition, the names of all the idols.

I think it was our stage manager, Auriol Lee, who finally persuaded Benny to stop going to the fights. She is about as green as you can be – if she had rats in her garden she would put food down for them, and she pilloried him for it. So he did eventually stop going. But I think it was really fear of public outrage that did the trick rather than suddenly seeing the light and recognizing the horror of it all. 'I know I'd be crucified if this got out, Den,' he finally admitted. However, he continued to watch bullfighting on TV whenever he was in Spain, right until the end.

He always liked to immerse himself as fully as possible into any country he visited. So imagine his feelings when we travelled to Los Angeles for talks with Hollywood producers and they proudly whisked us for dinner aboard the liner *Queen Mary*, which the Americans had bought and turned into a restaurant.

'I was brought up in Southampton docks and I spent half my life looking at that bloody thing,' he whispered to me. But he was actually very amused.

Our American hosts just wanted to make him feel at home. What he would really have preferred would have been to experience something – almost anything – typically American. If he could have chosen, he would probably have asked to go to a country and western bar or a jazz club or be driven out of town to some little place in the hills where he could arrive unannounced and just enjoy being somewhere different. That was Benny. The eternal traveller. Always wanting to experiment and to explore.

SEVENTEEN

FAMILY MONEY

Benny Hill's death, like his life, was veiled in a certain mystery and secrecy. The biggest mystery concerned his will and how Benny really intended to distribute his immense wealth. And now I can reveal the truth.

In the last days of his life he was writing a new, secret will. But it is not valid in law, because he died before he could complete it. So Benny Hill unwittingly left his £7.5 million fortune to members of his family who had died before him. He did this in a legally binding will, completed in 1961, which I am sure he had forgotten he had ever made.

I found the new, uncompleted will in Benny's flat shortly after his death. Benny's agent, his solicitor and I were going through the clutter trying to sort things out a bit. We were piling stuff in plastic supermarket bags, just the way Benny would have liked it really, when I came across a sheet of blue Basildon Bond writing paper covered in Benny's handwriting. It contained a list of names, and opposite each name was a sum of money. A very large sum of money.

The total amount listed was in excess of £2 million. I remember being vaguely aware that most of the names were of people Benny worked with, which, as his work was such an important part of his life, was only as one would expect. My own name jumped out at me. He had written an amount of money next to my name which would be a fortune to me.

I was a little overcome by the enormity of what I might have discovered and quickly handed this paper to the solicitor, saying: 'You may need this.' Having seen it, I have absolutely no doubt in my mind that it was meant to be Benny's will. But he had not signed it, and there were no witnesses. It was definitely in Benny's handwriting. Yet it has no validity in law without a witnessed signature. And so, because his mother and father and brother and sister, to whom he originally willed his money, were already dead, Benny's fortune is in the process of being divided among his nephews and nieces.

In spite of a great deal of inaccurate press speculation, the law on inheritance is actually quite simple. All the people named in his old will are dead. Therefore Benny's estate has to be split equally between their direct descendants – his brother's and sister's children. And in fact if Benny, as an unmarried man, had died without leaving any will at all, the end result would have been the same. If he had children, they would be the first claimants to his estate. Benny did not have children, therefore the estate would go to his parents. His parents were dead, so his brother and sister would stand to inherit. They too were dead, so the beneficiaries become his brother's and sister's children, Benny's seven nieces and nephews.

It is ironic that he hardly knew some of these relatives, who will now become extremely wealthy. There are the three teenage children of his sister Diana, who emigrated to Australia many years ago and died there in 1984 of leukaemia. Her sons Michael and Peter and daughter Tessa still live in Australia. Ben visited them occasionally on various trips down under, but never became close to them.

When they were growing up together in Southampton Ben adored his baby sister, eight years his junior. But when she grew up and after she married they drifted apart. Diana developed extreme left-wing views to a level which embarrassed Ben. It was during that time in the fifties and sixties when Communism was highly fashionable, particularly among young people. Ben was middle of the road, slightly to the right – in fact not all that interested in politics; but he was afraid of being publicly linked with Diana's Communist status.

He remained fond of her, yet he could not understand the kind of political animal she became. It was during his many working trips to Australia – where he made TV programmes and commercials – that he began to get to know his sister again, though the warm sibling relationship of their childhood was never renewed. When Diana became ill with the cancer which was to kill her Benny expressed concern across the world and sent offers of help, but he did not visit. And he did not go to her funeral.

Ben's brother Leonard, who died in 1990, left two daughters, Madeleine and Caroline, and two sons, Barnaby and Jonathon. Madeleine, who lives in Hove, near Brighton, has a severely hand-icapped daughter, Hannah, eight years old at the time of writing, on whom some of the money will be well spent. Benny would like the idea of his fortune helping a handicapped child, I am sure of that.

I am also sure that if in later years he had remembered his original will he would not have wanted it to stand. I think Benny signed it along with all sorts of other papers and just never gave it another thought. If he had, it seems likely he would have changed it for a number of reasons. His relationship with his sister Diana was sometimes strained, but any problems there paled into insignificance against the trouble there was between Ben and his elder brother, Leonard.

Ben and Leonard had a serious row which led to a rift between the two which lasted for seventeen years. It was a typical family fight, but it just didn't go away. The brothers did not speak for all that time. The split was very bitter, and although they were reunited a couple of years before Leonard's death in 1990 they never again became close. That was sad, because as little boys growing up in Southampton they were great pals – although Ben's cousin Chris Hill, who now lives in Waltham Chase near Southampton, remembers that the two were always scrapping even as boys.

Chris grew up near Benny's family home and recalls: 'We were all boys together and I used to go to stay with them. The brothers slept in one huge double bed and I used to have to sleep in it too. My auntie always put me in the middle, for some reason, and I used to be woken up by Len and Alfie throwing punches at each other.

'But they were close as lads, and it was a shame that there was such bitterness between them later. I never knew the details of their quarrel, but I did know that their parents took Alf's side.'

And that was why the family home in Southampton, in which Benny had been brought up from about the age of seven, was left to Ben. At the time of his mother's death the whole Hill family was in a rather sorry state in terms of their feelings towards each other. Mrs Helen Hill died estranged from her elder son Leonard. He did not go to her funeral, saying that he had been taken ill. And she shared Benny's misgivings about the behaviour of her daughter Diana. So I have always believed that, if Benny had remembered he had made a will naming Leonard, he would definitely have changed it during that long period when they were at loggerheads.

I also believe totally that Benny meant to leave a considerable sum of money to two handicapped ladies, both cerebral palsy sufferers, whom he visited frequently and who have already been mentioned. In a newspaper interview in December 1991, Benny described Phoebe King and Jeannette Warner as 'two very special lovely ladies.' He referred to them as 'my most loyal fans and closest friends' and said: 'Sadly all my family have gone now, so I must make a new will, and I can safely say that these two ladies will be number one and number two in it.'

That interview seemed to indicate that Ben was then aware of his earlier will, but I am not convinced. It sounds crazy, but making a will would be just the sort of thing he would forget. He was aware, of course, that his close next of kin to whom his estate would have automatically passed were dead. And so he was planning to do something about it at last. Benny also intended to leave sizeable chunks of money to a number of other people. I knew this even before finding that unfinished will among all those other scribbled-on pieces of paper in his flat.

And that leads to another reason why I reckon Ben had forgotten that document signed and witnessed way back in 1961. One night in a bar in New York he actually told me that he had no will. 'I must get round to making one,' he said. And then he started to list the people he cared about, those whom he would like to inherit his wealth. The two handicapped ladies were mentioned, as were many of the people Ben had worked with on his shows over the years. He did not mention my name, the old devil. But then, he wouldn't have done.

Strangely enough, the subject of Ben's will was a running joke between us and the rest of the team on the show. Ben's fear of heights – or any stunt that he considered dangerous, which was most of them – always led to me running forward with a piece of blank paper saying: 'Sign this – I'll fill in the details later.'

Ben always replied: 'You're getting nothing, Kirkland! I'm leaving it all to little Jackie.'

While all this was happening and Ben was shaking in his shoes I also used to shout: 'Right. Find the man who wrote this stuff!' Who, of course, was always Ben. We used the will joke on one occasion when Ben was genuinely terrified. He wrote a piece called 'The Loser' in which he was supposed to commit suicide. He had to plunge into a lake with a cartoon-size stone around his neck. Just before he jumps a fish is seen floating out, lifted by a balloon – it too is committing suicide.

To film Ben drowning we suspended him from a wire 100 feet up and he drifted to the supposed river bed alongside a treasure chest of gold – which he spotted too late to save himself. Ben had to pretend he was underwater and mime a man drowning – he did it brilliantly. I had shot through a fish tank and had planned to slow the film down to give a floating effect, but Ben's miming was so perfect I did not need to.

At one point I left him suspended 100 feet up and called 'lunch' – and the whole studio broke and left him hanging there. I had, of course, already got him to sign the usual blank piece of paper. That was the only time I have ever heard Ben use language that would make a sailor blush. But in spite of all the gags, when Ben really did start to make a new will – too late as it turned out – I was there on the list.

The main reason Benny did not get round to doing something about a new will until it was too late was bound to have been because of his disinterest in money and lack of awareness of it.

Top London agent Peter Charlesworth, Benny's friend since the mid fifties, remembers well Ben's curious attitude to money – how his natural frugality could be so easily mistaken for meanness, and yet how generous he was. 'I met Benny when I was plugging records and he was already a TV and radio star,' Peter recalls. 'We hit it off at once – one of the main things we had in common was that we were both great womanizers then. There came a time when I was down on my luck and Benny came to the rescue. He did a kind of deal with me – with Ben everything was a deal. I used to drive him around in my car and he would pay me far more than the going rate and buy me meals. It was geared to save my pride. He always talked about himself and me by name. He would phone me and say: "Charlesworth and Hill will go on an errand. Charlesworth will drive. Hill will buy lunch."'

On one of these errands Peter experienced that other, strange, penny-pinching side of Ben. 'He got me to take him to a warehouse in Paddington where they were selling tins of food which had come from a sunken ship. They had all lost their labels, so what you got was pot luck. Benny had seen it advertised that the stuff was going very cheaply and he couldn't resist it. He filled three sacks with these tins and then we went to his flat where he opened a selection of them and managed to cook a delicious lunch. He was earning about £1000 a week all those years ago – but, you see, he never really believed he had any money. He said he would need to see £1 million in a room to believe it was his.' It remains Peter's belief that there lies the real truth behind Benny's modest spending habits – right until his death he could never properly comprehend that he was an immensely wealthy man.

Yet he was quite shrewd. He employed an accountant and a stockbroker to handle things for him, and he left the day-to-day handling of his fortune to the experts. Knowing Benny, I am sure he kept a careful eye on what was going on, but he took no joy out of the possession of money in the way a lot of wealthy people do. He did not get involved in dabbling with investments himself. I never saw him buy the *Financial Times* or look at the money pages in any of the other more serious newspapers.

In fact the papers Benny loved were the tabloids. They were meat and drink to him, and his flat was invariably knee-deep in popular papers. He devoured the *Daily Mirror*, the *Sun* and the *Star* avidly. The *Express* and the *Mail* were a bit upmarket for him, but he usually bought those as well.

Money was simple to Benny. You either had it or you didn't, and he spent according to his needs rather than the dictates of society. 'I think you can safely say I spend less on myself than Zsa Zsa Gabor and rather more than Mother Teresa,' he once said.

He believed in using cash, not cheques or credit, which is unusual nowadays. But he did not carry round bundles of £50 notes in supermarket carrier bags as legend has it. Apart from his shopping, the plastic bags were used only for his notes and scripts – which were probably more valuable than a carrier bag stuffed with £50 notes.

Ben did not even possess a credit or charge card of any kind. He did not see the need for one. He always carried large amounts of cash with him, even if not in supermarket bags, and when he travelled abroad he took huge sums in travellers' cheques. I am pretty sure he did not even have a bank cheque card. Certainly I never saw him use one. I suppose people would usually just accept a Benny Hill cheque, and if he thought they wouldn't he would produce cash. Along with the Queen of England, he must have been one of the few people left in the world not to carry plastic.

He collected his immense wealth by accident. And his disregard for his huge income was demonstrated by the slapdash way in which he dealt with payments. Uncashed cheques were often tucked into drawers, as his old friend and first straight man Jeremy Hawk discovered on a visit to the Queens Gate flat. Asked to look out a pair of black socks for Ben, he found wads of cheques in the sock drawer, some over six months old. Ben himself told the story of how he received a letter about a commercial he had done and did not notice the cheque for £60,000 clipped to the back until it was pointed out by a colleague, who had appeared in the same commercial, when Ben remarked that he didn't think he had been paid yet.

'My agent complains that I'm always turning down the chance to make more money,' he once said in a newspaper interview, and went on:

But there's not a lot I can do with it. It's just something else to worry about. I get absolutely nothing out of money. It plays a secondary role in my life.

Once at the BBC I happily took a cut in wages so that they could spend more money on the show.

I don't want to be a showbusiness tycoon. I'm very much a status quo person. I like the way I am now. I don't want any more responsibilities.

My personal needs are very modest. I can't stuff myself with food because I get too fat. I usually eat in self-service places. Sometimes I buy a couple of shirts at £12 a time. Even when I'm lashing out I have a job spending £100 in one day.

That interview was conducted in the early eighties – before it became a national pastime to speculate on Benny's tight-fistedness. Later he became more sensitive about his spending habits and would mop his brow with handfuls of banknotes which he used to carry around with him in a jocular attempt to change his image.

Yet in spite of having pockets stuffed full of wads of £20 notes, multi-millionaire Benny Hill was once nearly arrested for stealing a £10 pair of cufflinks. In November 1991 we were going to the funeral of our friend and colleague Jack Brecken, who was Thames TV's legendary picture publicity boss for many years. We had to be in Bromley by 10 am on a working day in London, which meant a nightmare drive through all the rush hour traffic to get right across the city to the south of it. And it was the most vile day, pouring with rain and howling with wind, which always makes the traffic worse.

We left Teddington at 8.15 and were sitting in the back of this car when Benny said casually to the driver: 'If you happen to spot a gentlemen's outfitters would you stop, because I've got no cufflinks.'

Then I noticed that the cuffs of his shirt were hanging down out of his jacket sleeves. Typical Ben. If he didn't have a dresser to hand him everything he was always falling apart. Now, the problem with an incident like this when a star is involved is that you just can't get away with it. If I had been in the same situation I would just have said, 'To hell with it' and tucked the shirt cuffs up as best I could.

But this was going to be a funeral with a press presence, because Jack was a big showbiz man and a lot of celebrities were expected. So some pillock would have been sure to take a picture of Benny with his shirtsleeves dangling. The supermarket plastic bag saga loomed all over again. This time it would be the millionaire comic too mean to buy himself a pair of cufflinks. We could all do without that.

I said: 'Ben. You'll never ever find a gentlemen's outfitter's open before we get to Bromley, and where we are heading is not the kind of area where we're going to find one either.' But I knew we must get some cufflinks somewhere.

Anyway, mercifully the traffic was fairly kind to us and we reached Bromley by 9.30. We drove straight into the town centre, tore into two shops which didn't sell them and then spotted an Army and Navy store. Naturally the section which sold cufflinks was several storeys up and across the road along one of those linking corridors, and we were running the risk of offending several fans who spotted Benny because there was no way we could stop.

We snatched the first pair of cufflinks off a tray offered to us by a girl assistant. They cost £10.99 and Ben gave the girl £11 and we just ran. I was carrying in my hand the little box with the cufflinks in.

'Don't you want them wrapped?' she asked.

'No, thank you treasure, we're taking them straight out of the box and into his shirt,' I called back over my shoulder.

By then it was twenty to ten. We ran out of the shop, and as we set foot on the pavement this six-foot-three tall man stopped us. Apparently he was a trainee manager, I learned later.

'Excuse me, what are you doing with those cufflinks?' he said.

'Well, we've just bought them , and we're in a hurry because we've got to go to a funeral . . . .' I began.

Suddenly he had me in an armlock up against the wall. The time is ticking on, and to make matters worse it is still tipping down with rain and we are getting soaked.

I heard Benny whisper: 'Where's Jeremy Beadle?'

Then he did something I never saw him do before or after. He took off his glasses, turned full face to look at our assailant and said: 'I'm Benny Hill.'

It didn't help. Not one bit.

'Hmpf,' said this guy. No other reaction. Nothing. He threatened me with the police unless I stood still and waited, and he started to phone around the store to check our claim that we had bought the cufflinks. Eventually he tracked down the girl who had served us and we were released, but not with a very good grace. There was certainly no apology.

We were in a real panic. You can be late for a wedding, but not for a funeral. We did not stay to sort him out. We just fled, and we got to Jack's funeral with minutes to spare.

The next day I phoned the management of the Army and Navy store, who were terribly apologetic. I said I didn't want the guy sacked because he had made a mistake or anything like that, but I hoped everybody in the store would take the micky out of him unmercifully. 'Oh, they are already doing that,' I was told. 'He gets greeted with "'Allo Viewers" all the time.'

They sent me a formal letter of apology thanking Benny and me for taking such a reasonable attitude – after all, I suppose we could have sued them for thousands – and I thought that was the end of the matter.

But then I got a phone call from the *News of the World*. 'Is that the thief of Bromley?' the reporter addressed me.

Stupidly, when you consider what happened next, I asked them not to print the story because I thought this poor chap, whose name was Robert Doncaster, would probably lose his job. Then when I picked up the *News of the World* that Sunday there was this com-pletely distorted account of what had happened, all in the words of this blessed man Robert Doncaster whom I had been so concerned about. The headline read: 'Why I nicked Benny Hill . . . .'

And he had described us as scruffy and suspicious, which was a bit of a blow because neither of us had ever been so smart in our lives. We had our best suits on, shoes gleaming, shirt and tie immaculate – the lot. Of Benny, Doncaster said: 'He just looked like a small, scruffy, fat man in glasses.'

I had told him we were in a hurry to get to a funeral, and in the *News of the World* story Doncaster said: 'Neither appeared dressed for a funeral – Kirkland had on a beige coat.' I was deeply hurt. That 'beige coat' was four hundred quid's worth of Aquascutum raincoat. It was pouring with rain, and it so happens I don't have a black raincoat.

Finally the *News of the World* described Doncaster, rather curiously, as 'tall slim Robert, who has five O levels . . . .' This led to Ben saying: 'Hey, Den, when he had you up against the wall I should have asked him how many O levels he had, shouldn't I?'

We were tempted to make a fuss, but in the end we just laughed about it. I was known as Fingers Kirkland for a while and he was Benny the Bandit, but apart from that life went on as normal. I must admit it did seem a bit unlikely that a multi-millionaire superstar wouldn't have been able to come up with just one pair of cufflinks.

But that was Ben. Money, possessions meant so little. Not only has he left an estate worth £7.5 million – he has also left a staggering annual income from all his shows, which will probably soar to even greater popularity now he has died. Such is the way of the world.

I know there are all sorts of people around, in and outside his family, who expected to benefit from Ben's will had an up-to-date one been made. There have been countless stories in the papers about what will happen to his money. It's all been a bit of an undignified scramble, really. Ironic when you consider that Benny Hill really could not have cared less about his millions.

For myself, well, he did leave me a legacy. He left me a legacy of friendship, irreplaceable experience of working with one of the world's greatest comics, and many memories of great times. I should be so lucky to have worked not only with Ben, but also with the likes of Tommy Cooper, Frankie Howerd and Eric Morecambe, and to have been their friend. I am a lucky geezer. Ben would only hope that none of the knowledge I have gained is wasted.

EIGHTEEN

DEATH OF A COMIC

I knew he was dead as soon as I got the phone call from Benny's neighbours. I had half known, really, before the call came. But I did not want to face up to the thought that my best friend had died. I found Ben's body. He had already been dead for two days and it was the worst experience of my life. I had loved him so much and suddenly he was no longer there.

Ironically, just weeks before his death Benny had turned down an option which might have saved his life. He had been told he could have a heart bypass operation. If successful, it would restore his heart to 100 per cent health. But at his age there was only a 70 per cent chance of survival.

Ben explained this to me after coming out of hospital the second time. And he said: 'I'm not taking the risk, Den. I would rather slowly build myself up. I'll be all right.' Sadly, he was not all right. He never got the chance to build himself back to fitness.

The first indication that there was anything wrong with Benny came in early February 1992. He had not been feeling well for almost a week when he phoned me and said he was suffering from breathlessness and couldn't understand it. I called him back the next day, which was a Sunday. He said he was still feeling rotten, that he planned to visit his doctor the next day and had a feeling he might be put in hospital for tests.

On the Monday afternoon he phoned from the Cromwell Hospital. He told me which room he was in, that he had been whisked straight there, and asked me if I could bring him in a spare shirt and a pair of pyjamas and one or two other things. I picked up what he wanted and went along to visit him. That was when I learned that he had already had a minor heart attack.

Now, there is no such thing as a good heart attack – every heart attack is serious. But Benny's first one was the kind which is generally regarded as a slap on the wrist. After it you lose weight and generally change your eating habits and your lifestyle and with a bit of luck you will last a good few years more.

It wasn't a main artery attack. There had been no collapse or anything like that, and he didn't really know he had had a heart attack. He thought he had the flu – his chest and throat were full, and he couldn't catch his breath. He didn't have pains in his chest or anything like that. So, although we were all very anxious about him we weren't desperately worried. One of the biggest worries was trying to prevent a lot of fuss. That was impossible, of course, because the world's press very quickly picked up the news that Benny was in hospital and they all wanted to know what was wrong with him and how he was.

We were just on the verge of completing the deal with Central which would put Benny back on British TV with a new series for the first time in three years. I did not want to jeopardize that, and I also wanted to keep the pressure off him as much as possible.

He hated fuss about his health. When in 1976 he had to have that kidney removed he just told me he was going into hospital for his annual check-up. Then he phoned me and said he had had a kidney out. He said he didn't want me to worry. I was amazed. And later I learned that he had planned to delay the operation because we were due to start filming the show. He only had it when he did because rehearsals had been postponed for a few weeks.

So at first I am afraid I fibbed to the press and gave them the same sort of line all those years later: that Benny had gone into hospital for routine tests and the doctors wanted him to have a good rest, or some such nonsense. It didn't work, of course. The truth was soon out, but so thankfully was Benny. The medical team were pleased with him and he was released from hospital on 18 February after an eight-day stay. I had no choice but to organize a press photocall on the day he was sent home, in the hope that he would then be left alone. In fact, as I related earlier, it more or less organized itself, as photographers had been waiting outside the hospital ever since Ben was admitted.

There were dozens of photographers there, pushing and shoving each other and Benny as well. But typically he gave the impression that he was feeling quite well and was in fine form, posing with the nurses, hamming it up in his Fred Scuttle hat.

I took Benny home myself and sat and chatted with him for a while, and he seemed fine. But a couple of hours later he phoned me and said: 'I'm not breathing well. I can't breathe.'

I said: 'For goodness sake get your arse out of there. Phone for a cab and get back to the Cromwell.'

He called his doctor and then did what I had suggested. So he was back in hospital within little more than a couple of hours of having left. This time, though, they sent him to the Brompton, which specializes in cardiac problems.

He thought he was having another attack, of course, but in fact he wasn't, although what did happen was very worrying. As I understand it, his heart attack had slowed the rate at which his blood was being pumped around and so his kidney started to make liquid. This water was settling on his chest, making it difficult for him to breathe. And because he only had the one kidney the problem was more acute, apparently, than it would otherwise have been.

The doctors put him on a course of tablets to get rid of the water on his chest, but they had to be terribly careful because with just the one kidney there was no margin of error. He stayed in hospital for about a week that second time, and although he was feeling pretty poorly for most of the time he made the effort to visit other patients whom he knew were asking for him. He would sit down and talk to people who seemed to have far worse problems than him and give them a bit of Fred Scuttle or whatever.

By the time he left the Brompton seven days later they seemed to have really sorted him out. When he went home he looked better than he had since the problem began. The first thing he did when he walked into his flat was to seek out some videotapes and pack them up to send to a young boy he had met in hospital who was a great fan. This lad was a real charmer, bright as a button, but he had had some awful operation on his head for a tumour and had a very uncertain future.

Ben wasn't right, wasn't quite himself. He was tired and he was slow, and I could see that he was far from well. But we thought it would just be a matter of time and good sense to get him back to normal, and I encouraged him to think that way. However less than a couple of weeks later, on 8 March, Ben readmitted himself to the Brompton. Once again, he thought he was having another attack. In fact, apparently, it was really a kind of panic attack, which often happens to patients in a heart scare situation. But the man was obviously very poorly and was kept in for another five days.

On the 13th he was released again – there was very little further treatment he could be given except the major surgery he had rejected. We believe he died on Saturday, 18 April. It was two days later that I found his body. . . .

The doctors hadn't put Ben on a special diet, but they had told him to keep watching those calories and to take things very easy for a bit. Walking, his great love, was a good idea, they said. But not the way he walked before the attack, when he would go off on ten- or twelve-mile hikes. He was told to start from scratch, just gently strolling a few hundred yards at first, and slowly building up until he was fit again.

I used to go around most days and do his shopping for him, because he couldn't really manage that for himself. He was afraid he'd walk about three hundred yards, have to sit down on a wall and then it would rain and he would be wet through to add to all his other problems.

We discussed this at the very beginning on his first day out of hospital, and I said he wasn't to worry about the shopping. So he thrust a wad of money into my hand, and I just put in in my pocket thinking it was fifty quid or so. I didn't even look. Later I discovered it was mostly £50 notes neatly stacked from the machine – he'd given me more than 500 quid, the daft bugger, for a few fish fingers and the odd loaf of bread!

We spoke on the phone every day. The rule was that he would call me at 10 am every day. If it was a quarter past I would have a go at him. Some days he didn't want to see me at all. 'You're boring, Kirkland. Sod off. I want to be on my own,' he would say.

The day I found his body was Easter Monday, and I hadn't heard from him for two days. I was beginning to be very worried. The Saturday had been such a lovely day, and Benny had seemed so well that I wasn't too bothered. I phoned a couple of times and got no reply, but I thought he had either wandered off somewhere or was ignoring the phone. He was quite capable of that. He and I had a secret ring so that we knew who was on the other end of the line. Ring, ring. Stop. Then ring again. But he didn't always want to speak to me either – that was Ben.

None the less, on the Sunday I fretted all day. But the sun was shining and I kidded myself that he had set off somewhere. I was on the verge of going round to his place, but something seemed to stop me. He hated people visiting him unexpectedly and I knew that. But the real truth was that I think I already knew what I was going to find. That it was all over. And I was afraid. I should have gone. I wanted to go. But I was afraid to go.

Early on the Monday morning Benny's neighbours called me. The lights were switched on and had been switched on all the previous day. The television set was also on and they could hear it quite clearly. They had a feeling something was wrong.

I went round and banged on the door, to no response. We started to discuss smashing the door in, but I didn't want to do that. I knew Benny would hate it. One of the neighbours said he had a ladder, and we took it round to the side of the building so that I could climb up on to the balcony on the second floor.

It was quite a feat for me, because I am terrified of heights. Only in circumstances as extreme as those would I ever consider climbing a ladder. I started to shake when I was two foot off the ground, and the higher I got the more this blessed ladder started to wobble. I looked down at a row of anxious, upturned faces all watching me, and I heard myself say: 'If he's died on me, I'll kill him.'

Now showbiz folk tend to be flippant in the face of tragedy. Maybe lots of people do. Making some silly joke is a kind of release of tension. So I was half smiling when I clambered over the balcony rail, and down there on the ground were all those people rolled up with laughter.

Perhaps at the death scene of Benny Hill, one of the greatest comics in history, it was not that inappropriate. After all, I knew he would have been having a good laugh if he had been there. For a start he was even more scared of heights than I was, and he would have enjoyed seeing me suffer.

As soon as I got on to the balcony I could see him through the window. Benny was sitting up on the sofa in front of the television. His favourite position. So he had died watching TV. Stupidly, the thought instantly crossed my mind that if he could have chosen the circumstances of his own death he would like to have gone that way. But it was far too soon. He still had so much laughter yet to give.

There were patio doors from the balcony leading into the living room, but they were locked. I just stood there for a minute looking at my old mate. At first I was not that shocked, because I didn't really have any doubts about what I was going to find. But I was stunned, I suppose.

Ironically, Benny was looking quite smart for a change. He was wearing blue trousers and a pink shirt. I vaguely thought he must have just come in from going somewhere. He looked comfortable. His shirt was undone, he had his shoes off, socks off, and the telly was still chuntering away. He had the teletext on – which, curiously enough, he would watch endlessly. He liked the viewers' criticisms of TV programmes that they publish.

There were two empty plates to the right and a couple of low-calorie drinks to the left of him. He had obviously settled in for a typical Benny evening. One of the plates was a bowl, and I think he had been eating cornflakes.

He had his head back. His glasses were still on. He hadn't fallen over at all and was sitting quite upright. His eyes were closed. I remember one of my first thoughts was that there was no twinkle any more – the twinkle had gone forever.

He had been there for two days, and after that amount of time the body starts to do funny things to you. The gases in your body expand. He barely looked like Benny any more. It was not a nice sight. But at the same time he did look peaceful. I believe he died very quickly and very peacefully, and that is a comforting thought.

In fact I think, and hope, that he may have dozed off sitting there in front of TV and that he may have had the heart attack which killed him while he was asleep. If he was lying back on the sofa dozing, with his head stretched backwards, that would explain why he had not slumped forwards as you might expect with something as violent as a heart attack.

I turned slowly away. There was no hurry. I shouted down to the neighbours: 'You'd better call the police.'

Then I just stood there on the balcony and waited. Benny's neighbour opened his kitchen window and leaned out and asked me if I wanted a drink. Lovely chap. Automatically I went into that marvellous gag out of *Cheers* which Benny and I used to run through.

'It's too early.'

'What, too early for a drink?'

'No. Too early for stupid questions. Of course I want a drink.'

He offered me a brandy, but I asked for a glass of wine. I actually remembered quite calmly that I didn't drink spirits any more – although what did it matter at a moment like that? The neighbour leaned across and passed me a glass of white wine, and I stood there sipping it and looking through the window at Uncle Ben. And I thought to myself, wherever he is now I bet he was laying bets after I discovered him on how long it would take me to have a glass of wine in my hand. And now he'll be up there saying: 'Didn't take you long, little heart, did it?' I thought.

The police seemed to be there pretty fast. They broke in and I could see them through the kitchen window. They bust a pane of glass and let me into the flat. The stuff in the papers about hundreds of thousands of pounds in cash and cheques lying around his body was all nonsense – in spite of being part of a newspaper article attributed to me. I think I know who was responsible for that, and I am very angry about it. There were a couple of small cheques for £150 or so each, and about £300 in cash. He had obviously emptied his pockets, like you do, and that was the sort of amount Benny would always have on him. But he was not surrounded by a small fortune in readies, and I have two policeman who were there who would swear to that.

I wanted to open all the windows, but I wasn't allowed to do so. But they let me go over to Ben and smooth his hair down. It was all sticking up. He had this great head of hair to the end, the lucky devil. It was fabulous, bountiful hair, but it was unruly and had a mind of its own. He was always wetting it to get it to stick down. So, hard as I tried to smooth it down, it wouldn't stay.

The police were brilliant. Super-efficient. Within minutes, it seemed, the undertakers were there and took everything over. The neighbour who had given me the glass of wine supplied me with the rest of the bottle. When everything was finished and it was time to go the police drove me home – not because of the wine, but because I had just ceased to function properly. I was numb with shock.

When we got outside there were already press photographers there. I have some experience of how fast the press can move, but I was surprised at their speed on this occasion. I learned later that, because we had called the police to break into the flat, police headquarters were then notified. They are then obliged to inform the press. Funnily enough, none of the press people there that night approached me when we walked out of the block of flats because they were not the regular showbiz people, and they didn't know who I was.

For the next few days everything was a blur. The phone never stopped ringing. There were calls from all over the world, and even at the time of writing some months later it is still crazy. We had calls from lots of British comics like Jim Bowen and Bob Monkhouse and Bruce Forsyth and Harry Secombe, and I just can't start to name all the names. In any case I can hardly remember.

The funeral was arranged by my wife and Benny's eldest niece, his brother Leonard's daughter Caroline, together with Benny's agents Richard Stone and his partner Linda Ronan. It was Caroline who told us that they planned to bury Benny in Southampton next to his mother and father. The family were sure that is what he would have wanted, and I reckon they were right. He loved and respected his parents, and there was nowhere else that I can imagine he would have preferred to be. It was appropriate, really, that he was buried in the town where he was born. Like completing the circle.

We decided to try to keep the funeral as small and private as possible, just for family and close friends, if only because the church at the cemetery where he was to be buried was very small. Then there would be a star-studded memorial service, all welcome, in September.

It was a sad and extraordinary day. During the morning the weather had been grey with patches of sunshine. But as Ben's coffin was lowered into the grave the heavens opened. There was the most ferocious thunderstorm I can remember in this country for a long time – thunder, lightning, hailstones, the lot. It was spectacular. I don't know what it meant, but the timing was remarkable. Ben would have approved.

One thing I know for certain is that Benny was not afraid of death. We talked about dying. We talked about most things. And he was one of the few people I have ever known who genuinely seemed to have no fear of death. We never discussed religion, and he never told me whether or not he believed in any kind of life after death – but he had no fear about it. What did terrify him, which I know is a common fear, was of something happening to him, like a severe stroke, which would make him a physical vegetable, while his brain was still working but unable to transmit his thoughts to anyone.

One day he said to me: 'You will shoot me if that happens, won't you, Den?'

I said: 'I'll shoot you now if you want. When was the last time your brain worked anyway?'

I responded the way he would have expected, with a gag. We indulged in a bit more banter of a fairly tasteless nature, but I knew that he meant what he said. He feared a living death – and at least he was spared that.

NINETEEN

BENNY AND ME – THE END

We were a good team, Benny and me. I always knew that, and so did he. He used to say that our relationship was like a marriage of many years' standing. Lots of arguments and no sex.

Ben sometimes gave me a hard time, but the trust and respect between us was absolute. He was also a wonderful micky taker. And you could never become too big for your boots with Benny around. Considering his great fame and fortune and his huge talent he really was very modest. Pedantic, yes. But he had very little sense of his own importance, and the chronic insecurity he suffered from in those early years in theatre never left him. Maybe because of all that he believed it to be almost a duty to keep everyone around him in their place too. There was no room for prima donnas on *The Benny Hill Show*.

And as far as I was concerned, that rule went for its star too. I would not stand any nonsense from Ben. In the early days when I became his director and producer at Thames he had a reputation for eating directors. People were kind enough to say that I tamed him and made him someone everyone was happy to work with.

I think the truth is that we just got on so well together. Unusual in a big star, Benny was always happy to tell a story against himself, which I liked. He once told me how he had travelled alone to Singapore and stayed in the super smart Raffles Hotel. Nobody recognized him anywhere – that is until he wandered, by mistake he stressed, into the red-light district. The city's prostitutes and famous transvestites gave him quite a fright. They mobbed him. They knew exactly who he was!

We were buddies from the start, and if Benny began to get a bit stroppy about something he would almost never be stroppy with me. When I came on the scene he would put his arm around me, take me to one side and say, 'Right then, nature boy, what are we going to do about this?' And we would work the problem out sensibly.

If Benny ever started to sulk I would say: 'OK. Are we going to sulk all afternoon or are you going to tell me what the problem is?'

Eventually Ben would come out of it, and the moods became less and less frequent.

I know Ben and I had tremendous influence over each other. My wife Mary says she can see the Benny Hill in me all the time. 'Ben has moulded Den's personality in the most profound way,' she apparently told a friend not long ago. 'I didn't realize until latterly, when I began to spend more time with Ben, how much of Den's humour, his funny little asides, his quips, his way of dealing with problems, were not really original Kirkland at all. So much had been gleaned from Ben over the years.' She said this behind my back, of course. But she is probably right. After all, once on a trip to America a fan came charging up to me and asked for my autograph. He had actually mistaken me for Benny. I remember thinking that I must lose weight. One way and another we were a pretty complete double act.

A couple of years ago in Daytona, Florida, Ben and I were strolling back to our hotel along the beach late at night when we heard live music coming from a German bar. Ben, who was always fascinated by any kind of live music, suggested we go and have a jar. The place nearly stopped when he entered – but the band carried on playing. Suddenly, at a tune he recognized, he said: 'Come on, our kid!' and dragged me to the microphone. We sang three numbers to a tumultuous reception. He was such an able harmonist that he made even me sound good. That sort of behaviour belied his reclusive label – but, I have to admit, it was unlike him.

Usually he referred to me as his alter-ego. I could do outrageous things in public which he could not because of his fame, and they were not in his nature anyway. I could say things to people and get a laugh which he would not have considered saying. But he loved me doing it. I then became the front man and took from his shoulders the weight of constantly being expected to perform. He used to say to me: 'You were dreadful last night. Well done, our Den.'

We had a lot of fun during recording of some new Benny Hill records just a couple of years ago at the famous Abbey Road Studios, home of the Beatles for so long. At one point, when the musical director called 'Letter B', I burst into the old Beatles' number: 'Let it be, let it be.' Ben took me to one side. 'I'll do the funnies,' he commanded – but he was chuckling.

Another occasion when he was unusually extrovert occurred when I was about to leave *The Benny Hill Show*, on which I was then employed as floor manager, to start my career as a director for Thames TV. We were recording my last show, and as usual I did the warm-up for the studio audience.

At the end of each show the audience had to wait for ten or fifteen minutes in their seats while the tape was checked just in case of technical problems. I would go into a routine to keep the audience amused, and sometimes Benny would join in with a funny little song or something to pass the time. On this occasion he walked up to me and interrupted me in full flow, took the microphone from me and started to address the audience.

'I don't usually make speeches but I just have to make a speech tonight to tell you about our wonderful Den and how he is going off to be a director and how much we all adore him and are going to miss him . . . ,' he began.

Now I was beginning to glow. This was heaven. The audience were all going 'ooh' and 'aah', and Benny just did not stop. He gave this great eulogy about how marvellous and talented and special and clever and loveable I was. And I am afraid I was revelling in it. I was thoroughly indulging myself in all this back-patting from the world's most famous comedian.

Finally Benny said: 'And now we have just a little taste of something nice for Den because we all love him so much.' On came a prop man with a bottle of champagne and a glass. Ben poured the bubbly for me and backed away.

I was standing there basking in my own glory when I became aware that the audience were starting to laugh. I turned around, and behind me the entire crew were lined up with buckets of water and soda syphons and custard pies and disgusting missiles of all kind.

'Oh, no,' I thought.

Then I heard a voice say: 'Just let me do the first one, lads.'

I turned around and there was Benny with the biggest custard pie of them all in his right hand, poised ready to throw it. His face was a picture. I had been so busy glorying myself to the audience that I had no idea what was going on behind me, and Benny loved it. He was beaming with satisfaction. And then, *pow*, *whack*. The pie caught me right between the eyes, and after that the whole studio let fly. I ended up in a real gooey mess.

He really had me going, the little devil. And as I headed for a shower and prepared to throw away the clothes I had been wearing, which were totally ruined, I had to admit that it had been a good ruse. It had been hilarious really. I think the audience enjoyed it as much as the show itself.

Our relationship was much the same on- as off-screen. It was fairly easy most of the time. I understood the loner side of him, which helped. It was always at Christmas that people started to feel sorry for him. Journalists were frequently asking him what he was going to do at Christmas, and the answer was invariably the same. He would stock up the fridge with all kinds of goodies which he normally denied himself and sit in front of his two televisions and three video-recorders watching TV non-stop right over the Christmas holiday.

'Please don't give 'em the sad clown line,' he pleaded with Hilary Bonner in one of the last press interviews before he died. 'There is no better way of spending Christmas that I can think of. I shall be happy as Larry. There is so much to watch. And one of the great things about Christmas is that with a bit of luck you don't get too many callers – either at the door or on the phone – because people are all busy with their families.'

At Thames there used to be almost an annual ritual. Light Entertainment boss Phillip Jones would invite Benny to spend Christmas with him and his family at his lovely Teddington home not far from Ben's flat. His agent Richard Stone also invited him. So did Sue Upton. And so, rather half-heartedly, did I. Every year he turned us all down. I was always half-hearted with my invitation because I was perhaps the only one who really knew and understood that the last thing Benny wanted was to be trapped in somebody else's home for two or three days of festivities. He was one of the few men I have met in my life who was genuinely happy with his own company almost endlessly. He had friends and he enjoyed their company – but only on his own terms. And that did not include the extreme sociability of Christmas.

Ben did indeed like to do everything his way. I remember meeting up with him one day for a pint at our Teddington local. He had been for an early morning appointment at his dentist in St John's Wood and walked all the way back. Now, not only is that about ten miles, it's also not a particularly pleasant walk. It's all main roads, noise and dust really. I thought he had gone stark staring mad and said so. But to Benny that was perfectly normal behaviour. He loved walking, and reckoned you saw things when you were on foot that you totally missed when using any other form of transport.

Seeing things and picking up ideas was so much a part of his life that it was just second nature. I began to think the same way after working with him for a bit. Once in a pub I watched this lovely little charade where two blokes were standing at a bar with their backs to each other and they had their pints of beer on the same mat. One of them pulled his pint along the bar a bit and the other bloke's pint came with it. The other bloke reached out for his pint and it wasn't there. So he got hold of the end of the mat and pulled, and then the first bloke's pint disappeared. Daft, really, but it was very funny to watch. So I told Ben about it, and he built an entire sketch around it. Once more I had earned his description of me as 'a writer's labourer'.

Those occasions when I gave Ben an idea, or he talked over an idea with me and I was able to throw it back at him and take it a bit further, were some of my best times with him. Of all the work we did together there was one sketch which was my favourite and Ben's too.

Ben was a clown who did a strip. First he stripped off his clothes, and then he became a skeleton on screen and he stripped off his bones. It sounds odd, but anyone who has seen it will surely remember it and know how brilliant it was. It was funny but poignant too. It was also very hard to do, and Benny was frightened of it. For two or three years we were going to do it and he put it off. Eventually I virtually had to force him to do it. He gave in because he knew it was a clever concept, but he knew how technically difficult it was going to be and he was afraid of not getting it quite right.

Well, we did get it right. In France they gave Ben a special award just for that sketch, they loved it so much. But it was very hard work. It wasn't fun to do. Ben and I had a lot of fun working together, but that sketch called for too much concentration and effort to be any fun at all.

We were always playing around with ideas. One that tickled Ben was the way television teaches you to drive. It teaches you to drive on two wheels, to scream around corners, to career on two wheels along pipes, and you must always pass a burning field – like in a recent TV commercial. The one thing you don't learn is how to drive along a road, because they never do, do they?

When Ben was working he retreated into his own private world. He had several nervous habits, the most unfortunate of which was that he would pick at the base of his nails until they bled. In order to stop himself doing this he covered the ends of his fingers in sticking plaster.

On one occasion he caused concern when he arrived in Australia and the waiting press corps homed in on what appeared to be his badly damaged hands. His fingers were wrapped in so much Elastoplast that they thought he had been in an accident. Ben sent me a clipping from a Sydney newspaper expressing this fear with a note saying: 'We know better, don't we, our Den?' You see, he called it Kirkland's Disease. Yes, I got the blame for everything.

When he was concentrating or concerned about anything he had a habit of humming loudly – usually a song called 'If It Takes for Ever', which he used to think was appropriate sometimes when we were changing the props.

Once when I sent him off to change I yelled after him: 'And stop humming!'

He replied: 'I'm not.'

So I shouted: 'Well, don't start!'

When he was thinking about characterization he could become so preoccupied that he did not notice at all what was going on around him. He told me of the time he was walking through a park trying to find a new voice for a character, a pompous head waiter. The voice he was looking for was to be a cross between W. C. Fields and an upper-crust Englishman. The joke centred around the menu and Benny, referring to pieces of chicken, of course, was walking along all alone saying, 'Nice plump breasts!' over and over again in different accents.

Unfortunately he became so carried away that he left the deserted park and without realizing it entered a busy main street. And his voice was growing louder and louder. With head down, looking neither left nor right, he suddenly discovered the voice he wanted. He lifted his head and shouted in triumph: 'Nice plump breasts!' The traffic stopped, and a passing cyclist crashed into a wall.

Benny and I worked together so well that the partnership became accepted as a fact of life even after we were sacked by Thames

– perhaps particularly then – both by us without thinking about it, and by anyone who was considering hiring Benny. I would have gone to Central as Ben's director had he lived. I know that was part of the deal. And when in 1991 BBC's *Omnibus* filmed a documentary about Benny, *Clown Imperial*, which was repeated at the time of his death, Ben insisted on getting me in on the act.

He was always worried about being himself and he was happier if I were there to make sure he was coming over the way I knew he would have wanted to. He was a creature of habit, Ben. And I guess I became a habit to him.

He used to like to have me around not just when he was making programmes, but also when he was giving interviews. He wasn't particularly good at press interviews, and he liked to have some moral support. But I couldn't stop him saying things that seemed to give the wrong impression. He would spend an entire interview explaining how his humour was not sexist and so on, and then make some quip about his alleged seduction technique which negated the whole thing. Few people ever seemed to grasp that it was all part of the performance. Then his act and his true personality would become all mixed up in the press. A much-quoted comment of Ben's when he was being accused of operating a casting couch for the Hill's Angels was: 'I can honestly say I have not been to bed with one of the Hill's Angels. I think her name was Sandra!'

Ben could never resist the gag of the moment. But a lot of his comedy involved pathos. The sadder sides of life were very much part of our humour in *The Benny Hill Show*. And in our shows, of course, we became masters at altering reality to get laughs. We would reverse prints and use double speed and edit out the dull bits.

Benny used to say: 'Wouldn't it be lovely if life could be like a television show? Then you could cut out the bad bits or double speed them so that you get them over with quickly, and slow down all the nice things that happen to you.'

Benny wrote a song once which was a Bob Dylan micky-take, which he was very fond of doing – not because he didn't like Bob

Dylan, but because with all that wailing and moaning the lad lent himself beautifully to having a bit of fun poked at him. The song was called 'Please Can I Go Round Again?' It was about a little boy who discovers his first fairground, and in this fairground is a roundabout. Benny, being the clever writer that he was, made it the roundabout of life. So whenever something lovely happened to the boy he asked: 'Please can I go around again, ma?'

Ben sang it first of all on the show. He did his over-the-top Bob Dylan impersonation and the poignancy barely came across at all. Then, as recently as 1991, he recorded 'Please Can I Go Round Again?' as part of a CD of his work called *Benny Hill, The Best Of*. Once again he parodied Bob Dylan and sang it as a comedy number, albeit a gentle one.

Then one morning I happened to pick up a copy of the lyrics and read them. It was only then that I realized how very beautiful and moving the words were.

Benny was fighting fit when he composed the song, and he did not intend it to be his own epitaph. Had he done so, even he could not have come up with a better one.

At the end of the song the little boy, now an old man, is on his deathbed and says:

> *I don't believe that I'll never see your skies or your trees again,*
> *The women were fine, and so was the wine,*
> *And I shouldn't complain; but then,*
> *You give such damn short rides in this fairground of yours, Lord,*
> *Please may I go round again?*

INDEX

INDEX